CRAFTING FOR GIRLS

CRAFTING FOR GIRLS

35 EASY PROJECTS YOU'LL LOVE TO MAKE

**Charlotte Liddle
and friends**

CICO kidz

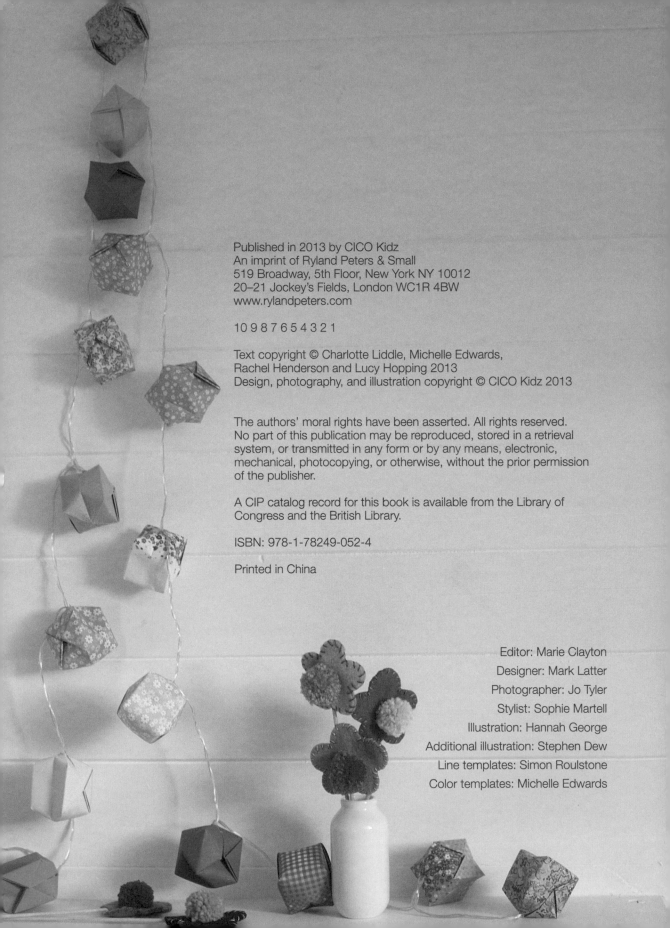

Published in 2013 by CICO Kidz
An imprint of Ryland Peters & Small
519 Broadway, 5th Floor, New York NY 10012
20–21 Jockey's Fields, London WC1R 4BW
www.rylandpeters.com

10 9 8 7 6 5 4 3 2 1

Text copyright © Charlotte Liddle, Michelle Edwards,
Rachel Henderson and Lucy Hopping 2013
Design, photography, and illustration copyright © CICO Kidz 2013

A CIP catalog record for this book is available from the Library of
Congress and the British Library.

ISBN: 978-1-78249-052-4

Printed in China

Editor: Marie Clayton
Designer: Mark Latter
Photographer: Jo Tyler
Stylist: Sophie Martell
Illustration: Hannah George
Additional illustration: Stephen Dew
Line templates: Simon Roulstone
Color templates: Michelle Edwards

CONTENTS

INTRODUCTION

Crafting has always been a huge passion of mine—even as a young girl I was always fiddling around designing or making something. I was often given craft kits as birthday or Christmas gifts and spent most of my school vacations making jewelry, modeling with clay, drawing and sticking, sewing clothes for my dolls, and trying to work my knitting machine (I never did have much success with that). I loved everything about the whole process, from conjuring up weird and wonderful ideas to actually making them happen. I enjoyed the freedom I had as a child because nobody really expected that much of my creations, yet I seemed to have a natural talent and was often complimented on the things I made. This spurred me on to continue my studies into art, design, and textiles and I am now lucky enough to have a career doing something that I really love.

During my time at university and working in the textile industry I have made three good friends—Lucy, Michelle, and Rachel—who are also very talented designers. So when I was asked to write a book aimed at young people, I was quick to enlist the help of my friends to create a range of mixed craft projects that are fun and a little bit frivolous.

Together we have come up with a range of projects based around techniques such as knitting, felting, sewing, embroidery, and papercrafting. The book

features three different chapters: **For Your Bedroom**, which shows you how to make personalized photo pillows, dream catchers from old doilies, magnetic makeup boards, and much more. If you enjoy dyeing or customizing your own clothes and shoes, or upcycling jewelry, then the **Clothes and Accessories** chapter will give you lots of ideas. It is jam-packed with new and innovative techniques and materials such as shrink plastic, which is a brilliant and quick way to make your own fashionable necklaces and rings. **Party Time** is the final chapter, which is full of fun crafting ideas for party decorations and invitations. Each project has a skill level

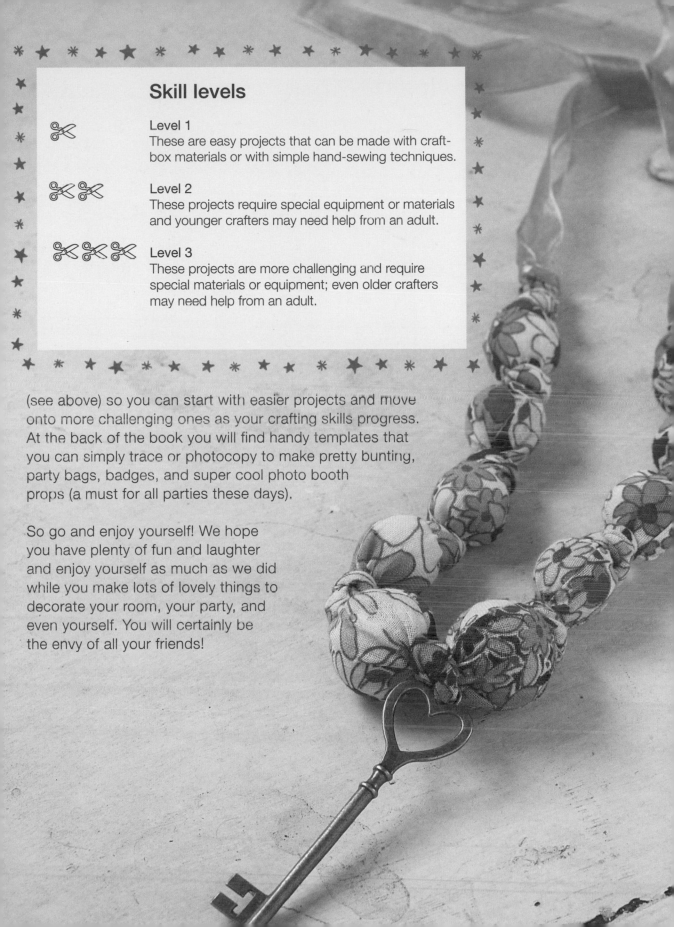

Skill levels

Level 1
These are easy projects that can be made with craft-box materials or with simple hand-sewing techniques.

Level 2
These projects require special equipment or materials and younger crafters may need help from an adult.

Level 3
These projects are more challenging and require special materials or equipment; even older crafters may need help from an adult.

(see above) so you can start with easier projects and move onto more challenging ones as your crafting skills progress. At the back of the book you will find handy templates that you can simply trace or photocopy to make pretty bunting, party bags, badges, and super cool photo booth props (a must for all parties these days).

So go and enjoy yourself! We hope you have plenty of fun and laughter and enjoy yourself as much as we did while you make lots of lovely things to decorate your room, your party, and even yourself. You will certainly be the envy of all your friends!

TECHNIQUES

In this section, we've provided you with a simple guide to everything you need to know to make the projects in this book, with step-by-step instructions for both sewing and knitting techniques. You could practice first on scrap pieces of fabric or with spare yarn if there are any stitches you're unsure of and want to improve before you use them for one of the projects.

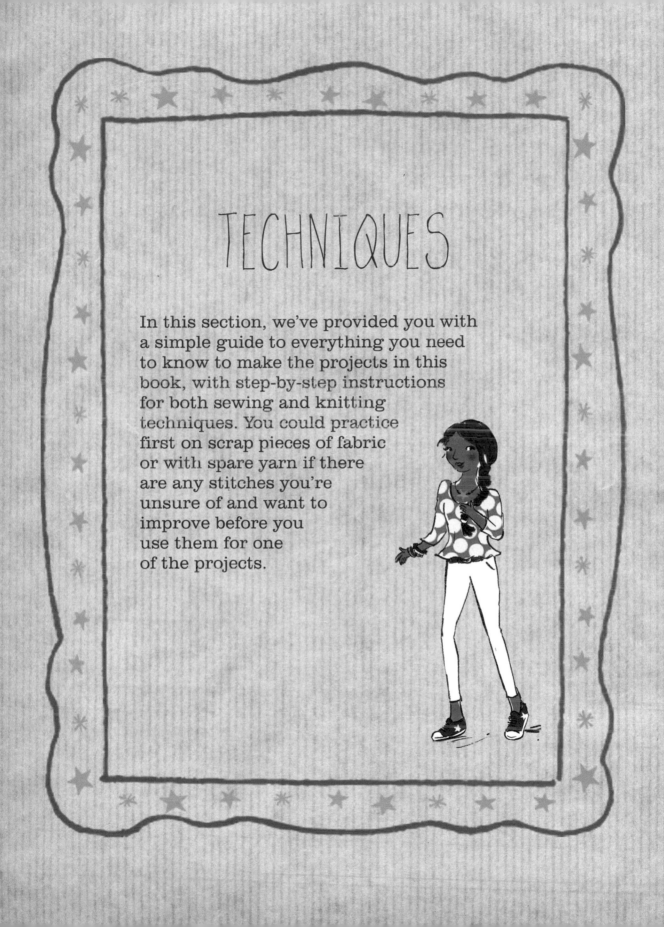

GENERAL CRAFTS

Stamping
Stamping is a very easy and quick way to create a design. Simply press a rubber stamp onto an ink pad and then press the stamp straight onto the surface you want to decorate. If you are using paint rather than ink it is a good idea to use a paintbrush to apply the paint onto the stamp. For a nice neat finish, clean any excess paint or ink from around the edges of the stamp to avoid printing marks that are not part of your design.

Gluing
PVA or fabric glue is a quick way to stick two pieces of paper or fabric together. The main thing to remember when using glue is that you should use a brush to apply it and make sure that you do not use too much—excess glue can sometimes squirt out from the edges, which may well make an unsightly sticky mark on your design.

Copying/enlarging templates
The easiest way to copy or enlarge the templates in this book is to use a photocopier, or printer/scanner, which usually have a percentage (%) button to control how big or small you can make the image. To enlarge the image just increase the percentage button to the figure given on the template.

Cutting out
Always use a clean, sharp pair of scissors. Keep separate fabric and paper scissors, because cutting paper with fabric scissors will quickly blunt them. When cutting fabric make a few big cuts rather than lots of little cuts; this will give you a smoother cut edge.

SEWING

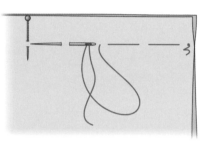

Securing the thread end
At the start of your stitching, and when you have finished sewing, secure the thread end by sewing a few tiny stitches over and over in the same place on the back of the fabric. Then trim off the end of the thread.

Basting (tacking)
Long, straight stitches, usually made by hand within the seam allowance, are used to hold layers in place temporarily during construction but are removed after the final seam is stitched. On fine or slippery fabrics the stitches can be made smaller and more even in size.

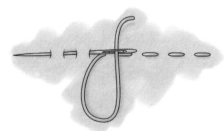

Running stitch
A long, straight stitch made by hand, used to gather fabric or as a decorative stitch. For gathering, the stitches should be fairly loose so they can be drawn up to gather the fabric evenly.

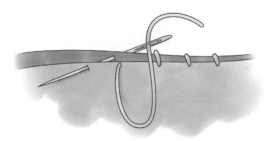

Oversewing

This stitch is used to close openings. With the edges together, bring the needle out through one folded edge, pick up a few threads from the other side of the opening, and then thread it back into the first folded edge. Continue along the opening, drawing the two sides together as you work.

Satin stitch

Work straight stitches very close together, working to the outline of the shape and keeping the edges even. You may prefer to draw the shape onto the fabric first; if so, ensure that your stitches are worked to the outside of the line so it does not show.

Back stitch

Back stitch is a very useful stitch because it gives the effect of a continuous line.

1 Bring the thread up through the fabric then work a stitch backward. Go down through the fabric and underneath, and come up a stitch length in front of the last stitch.

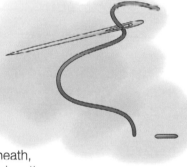

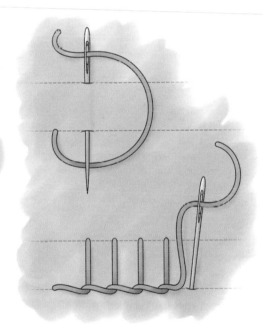

2 Work the next stitch backward to meet the end of the first stitch worked, again coming up a stitch length in front. Repeat to make a continuous line of stitching.

Blanket stitch

Bring the thread out through the fabric at the top of the stitch. Take a vertical stitch through the fabric a short distance away and then loop the thread around the tip of the needle and pull it through. Take the next stitch the same way, making sure to keep the vertical stitches all the same length and the same distance apart.

Sewing on buttons

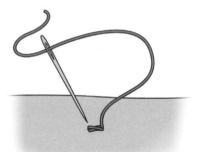

1 Mark the place where the button is to go. Push the needle up from the back of the fabric and sew a few stitches over and over in the marked place to secure the thread end.

French knot
French knots make little beads of thread on the surface of the fabric.

1 Knot the thread and bring the needle up from the back of the fabric to the front. Wrap the thread once or twice around the tip of the needle, then push the needle into the fabric, right next to where it came up.

2 Bring the needle up through one of the holes in the button and then back down through the second hole and into the fabric. Repeat this five or six times—don't pull the thread too tight because there needs to be some room between button and fabric. If there are four holes in the button, use all four of them to make a cross pattern. Keep the stitches close together under the middle of the button.

2 As you push the needle through, hold the wrapped threads tight against the fabric with the thumbnail of your other hand. Pull the needle all the way through so the wraps form a small knot on the surface of the fabric.

Sewing on beads and sequins
To stitch on a sequin with a bead, bring the thread up through the fabric then thread on the sequin and tiny bead. Take the thread over the bead and back down through the hole in the sequin. Single beads are sewn on in the same way, omitting the sequin.

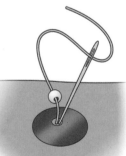

Machine sewing

Some of the projects will be quicker and easier if you make them on a sewing machine. You may need an adult to help you set up the machine and get you started but it won't be long before you can stitch straight seams by yourself.

1 Prepare the bobbin and thread the machine with the right sewing thread for your project.

2 Check that you have selected a straight stitch in the correct size.

3 Raise the presser foot and the needle and place the fabric underneath, lining up the edge that you want to sew with the edge of the presser foot—this will give you a seam of about ¼ in. (5 mm).

4 Lower the presser foot and start to stitch by pressing on the foot pedal. To keep your seam straight, keep the edge of the fabric lined up with the edge of the presser foot and gently guide the fabric away from you with one hand at the front, and hold the fabric as it moves out at the back. Don't pull it! The machine will keep the fabric moving, you just need to keep it in a straight line. If you have pinned the seam, remove the pins before they pass under the needle.

5 When you come to the end, select the reverse stitch button and stitch a few stitches backward and forward to secure the thread. Raise the presser foot and pull the fabric away with the threads still attached. Cut the threads about 4 in. (10 cm) from the needle. You have now stitched a seam!

You may need some adult supervision when using a sewing machine.

SEWING **13**

Machine zigzag

Most sewing machines can be adjusted to stitch different types of zigzag stitch. The stitch length controls how close together the stitches will be, while the stitch width controls how wide the zigzag line will be. Sew a few test lines of stitching before using it on your project. If the zigzag is being stitched around appliqué, keep the stitch length very short so you will have a fairly solid line, like a machine version of satin stitch.

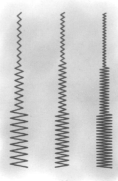

Tying a bow

Take hold of the middle of the ribbon and make a loop, holding it with your finger and thumb. With your left hand take the left side of the ribbon over the top of your thumb backward. Now pull the ribbon through the loop you have made over your thumb. Pull both loops of the bow firmly to make it secure.

Using Bondaweb

Bondaweb is a quick and easy way to attach fabric motifs securely to the main fabric, ready to add zigzag stitching or embroidery.

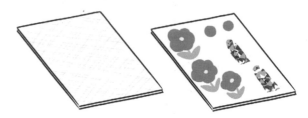

1 Place a piece of Bondaweb rough side down onto the wrong side of the motif fabric and iron in place over the paper backing, following the directions on the Bondaweb packet. Turn the fabric right side up and cut out motifs from the pattern on the fabric, or cut shapes using a template.

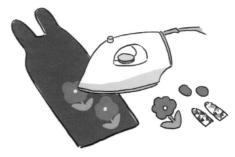

2 Peel away the paper backing from the cut shapes and place them right side up onto the right side of the main fabric. Use an iron to fix the shapes in place following the directions on the Bondaweb packet.

You may need some adult supervision when using Bondaweb.

KNITTING

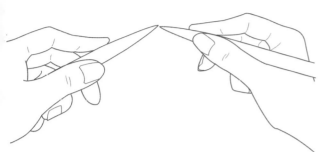

Holding needles

Pick up the left needle with your left hand, supporting it with your finger lightly resting on the top. Pick up the right needle as you would a pen with the needle resting in the crook of your thumb. Hold it approx. 1 in. (2.5 cm) from the tip of the needle. As you start knitting this hand will gently move up toward the tip of the needle and back down again.

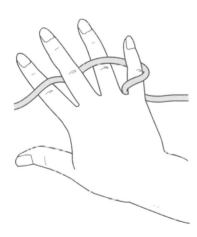

Holding yarn

Hold both needles in the left hand while picking up the yarn in the right hand. Pick up the strand of yarn with the ball on your right. With the right hand, catch the strand of yarn with your little finger with your palm toward you, then turn your palm over lacing the yarn over the third, under the middle and over the first finger of the right hand.

Making a slip knot

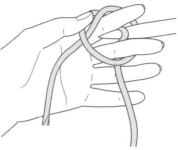

1 Wrap the yarn loosely around the first two fingers of your left hand, crossing the yarn over once. Place a needle under the back strand of the yarn and pull through to make a loop on the needle.

2 Gently slip your fingers away from the loop and lightly pull the end on the left to tighten the knot. It should be firm on the needle but not so tight that you can't fit the other needle through it.

Casting on

There are a few methods of casting on but the one used for the projects in this book is the cable method, which uses two needles.

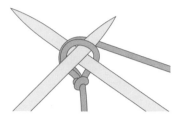

1 Make a slip knot as outlined on page 15. Put the needle with the slip knot into your left hand. Insert the point of your other needle into the front of the slip knot and under the left needle. Wind the yarn from the ball of yarn around the tip of the right needle.

2 Using the tip of your needle, draw the yarn through the slip knot to form a loop. This loop is your new stitch. Slip the loop from the right needle onto the left needle.

3 To make the next stitch, insert the tip of your right needle between the two stitches. Wind the yarn over the right needle, from left to right, then draw the yarn through to form a loop. Transfer this loop to your left needle. Repeat until you have cast on the right number of stitches for your project.

Knit stitch

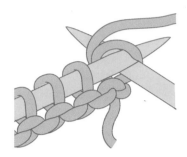

1 Hold the needle with the cast-on stitches in your left hand, and then insert the point of the right needle into the front of the first stitch from left to right. Wind the yarn around the point of the right needle, from left to right.

2 With the tip of your right needle, pull the yarn through the stitch to form a loop. This loop is your new stitch.

3 Slip the original stitch off the left needle by gently pulling your right needle to the right. Repeat these steps until you have knitted all the stitches on your left needle. To work the next row, transfer the needle with all the stitches into your left hand.

Purl stitch

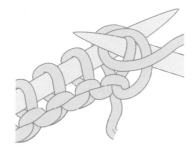

1 Hold the needle with the stitches in your left hand, and then insert the point of the right needle into the front of the first stitch from right to left. Wind the yarn around the point of the right needle, from right to left.

2 With the tip of the right needle, pull the yarn through the stitch to form a loop. This loop is your new stitch.

3 Slip the original stitch off the left needle by gently pulling your right needle to the right. Repeat these steps until you have purled all the stitches on your left needle. To work the next row, transfer the needle with all the stitches into your left hand.

Gauge (tension)

Gauge (tension) means how loose or how tight you knit. To achieve the exact measurements of a pattern you need to work to the same gauge as that recommended in the gauge guide or your project will come out a different size. Some patterns don't give a gauge guide, particularly if it's for a small item such as a purse or bag, but a gauge guide is particularly important if you're knitting a garment.

You can easily measure your gauge by knitting a square in the same stitch given in the pattern, and with the needle size that is recommended. Your gauge square should be at least 6 x 6 in. (15 x 15 cm).

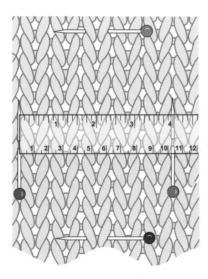

When you have finished your square, lay it flat and measure the number of stitches and rows over a 4 in. (10 cm) square. Either use a transparent ruler and count the stitches and rows to the length, or use a tape measure and place pins to mark out the 4 in. (10 cm) square and then count the stitches and rows between the pin markers. If the number of stitches and rows is less than the number specified in the pattern, your project will be too big. Change to smaller needles until you achieve the correct gauge. If the number of stitches and rows is more than the number specified in the pattern, your project will be too small. Change to larger needles until you achieve the correct gauge.

Knit 2 together (K2tog)

Using the right-hand needle, knit two stitches together knitwise and then slip them both off the left-hand needle.

Binding (casting) off

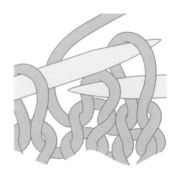

With the yarn at the back, knit two stitches. Using the tip of the left-hand needle, lift the first stitch over the second stitch and off the needle. Knit the next stitch and continue as before until only one stitch remains. Cut or break the yarn, pull the tail end through the loop and pull gently to secure the last stitch.

Sewing in ends

To tidy up yarn ends, thread them into a yarn needle and run a few small stitches forward then backward through the knitting, in a seam if possible. Trim off the remaining end.

Knitting abbreviations

These are the knitting abbreviations that you will need to know to follow the instructions in this book.

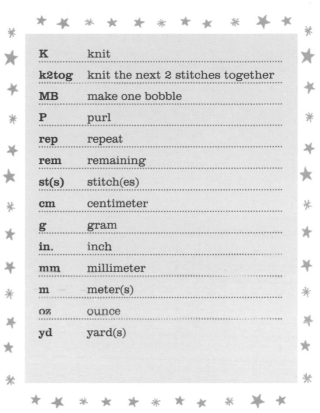

K	knit
k2tog	knit the next 2 stitches together
MB	make one bobble
P	purl
rep	repeat
rem	remaining
st(s)	stitch(es)
cm	centimeter
g	gram
in.	inch
mm	millimeter
m	meter(s)
oz	ounce
yd	yard(s)

Stockinette (stocking) stitch

To make this stitch, you work alternate rows of knit and purl stitches. The front of the fabric is the side when you work the knit rows. This stitch is used for the main part of the hats and other projects in this book.

[ ] Square brackets are used around instructions that you need to perform more than once. For example: [k2tog] 3 times means that you need to knit two stitches together three times.

( ) When you have worked a row to increase or decrease the number of stitches on your needle, the number of stitches you should have after completing the row is given in round brackets at the end. For example: (6 sts) means that you should have six stitches on your needle. Round brackets also give the alternative stitch counts or row counts for different sizes. For example: K6(8) would mean you knit 6 stitches for the smaller size and 8 for the larger size.

CHAPTER 1
FOR YOUR BEDROOM

This chapter is full of inspiring ideas for your bedroom. Projects featured in this section include a fabric lampshade, cool collage coasters, a magnetic makeup board, and some fun stationery ideas such as the bunny pencil case or felt pencil toppers. If you are a beginner you may like to try the simple pompom decorations, soaps, or candles. If you enjoy a challenge then have a go at the photo pillow or pencil case.

UPCYCLED LAMPSHADE

Upcycle a tired old lampshade with strips of funky fabric, then embellish it with beads and sequins.

YOU WILL NEED

Hexagonal or square lampshade frame

Scissors

Approx 20–25 strips of fabric, ribbon, and braid, each about 36 x ¾ in. (90 x 2 cm)

Assorted beads and sequins

White sewing thread

Needle

Lamp base and bulb

Spray paint (optional)

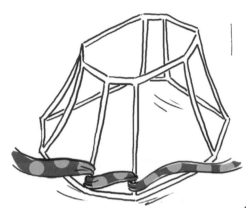

1 Strip off the old fabric cover of the lampshade frame and clean away any scraps of glue left on the framework. Take the first fabric strip and weave it around the spokes of lampshade frame.

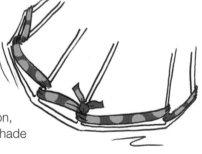

2 Once you have gone all the way around, tie the ends in a tight knot and trim off the excess fabric. Repeat with the other strips of fabric, ribbon, and braid until your lampshade is covered.

TIPS

If you cannot find a suitable old lampshade and base, buy an inexpensive new one to customize.

An ugly lamp base can be smartened up with a coat of spray paint, or you may want to spray it in a new color to match the lampshade.

3 Stitch sequins and beads at random onto the fabric strips. Try to place them on contrasting colors of fabric or ribbon so they show up. Assemble the lampshade, base, and lamp bulb back together and it is ready to use!

PHOTO PILLOW

This pillow provides a brilliant way of displaying photos of fun times with your friends! You can add embellishments with ribbon and buttons, as I have done, or let the photos be the main decoration.

Skill Level ✂ ✂ ✂

YOU WILL NEED

Selection of photographs, saved digitally

2 sheets of heat transfer paper in a dark color

Scissors

16-in. (40-cm) square piece of denim fabric

Baking paper or silicone sheet

Iron

Sewing machine and thread

4 strips of Bondaweb, each 12⅝ x 2⅜ in. (32 x 6 cm)

4 strips of lace trimming, each 12⅝ x 2⅜ in. (32 x 6 cm)

8 x 8 in. (20 x 20 cm) Bondaweb

8 x 8 in. (20 x 20 cm) star pattern fabric

Selection of buttons, beads, and sequins

Ribbon

16 x 22 in. (40 x 55 cm) denim fabric

Tape measure

15 in. (38 cm) square pillow pad

1 Print out the photographs onto the two sheets of heat transfer paper, following the manufacturer's instructions. Cut the images out and peel off the backing paper.

You may need some adult supervision for Steps 2, 3, and 4.

2 Arrange the images in the center of the square of denim fabric. Place the baking paper or silicone sheet over the top and press with an iron to fix the images in place, again following the manufacturer's instructions. Use a sewing machine to work zigzag stitch around each of the photographs.

3 Place the strips of Bondaweb onto the back of the lace strips and press with the iron to attach, following the instructions on the Bondaweb packet. Peel away the paper backing and place the lace trimming strips around the edges of the photomontage as shown in the diagram. Press again to fix in place, following the instructions on the Bondaweb packet.

4 Attach the square of Bondaweb to the wrong side of the star fabric as explained in Step 3. Cut out a selection of stars, peel off the paper backing and arrange the stars at random around the photomontage. Press to fix the stars to the denim. Stitch on a selection of buttons, beads, and sequins. Tie the ribbon into a bow and stitch in place.

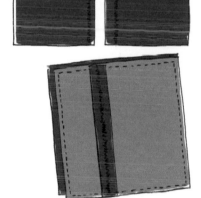

5 Cut the rectangle of denim in half to make two pieces 16 x 11 in. (40 x 27.5 cm). Fold under by ⅜ in. (1 cm) along one long edge on each piece, with wrong sides together. Machine zigzag along each edge to hold the hem in place. Place the pillow front face up on a table and place the two backing pieces on top right side down, with the hemmed edges overlapping in the middle but the outer edges in line with the edges of the front of the pillow. Machine stitch around all four sides ⅜ in. (1 cm) from the edge and then turn right side out through the envelope back. Insert the pillow pad through the envelope back.

DREAM CATCHER

Keep any nightmares at bay with this bright and cheerful dream catcher that you can hang up by the window or on the door. Even if you don't have nightmares, at least your bedroom will look fabulous!

1 Wrap lengths of each different color yarn around the wooden ring, threading through the loop of yarn each time as shown in the diagram. This will make a line of knots on the ring to hold the yarn wrap in place. Keep on wrapping until all the wood is covered.

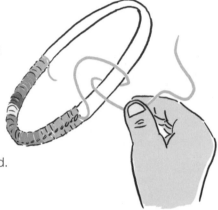

2 Lay the crochet doily onto the ring and use the needle and thread to stitch the crochet onto the yarn wrapping. Use small stitches so they will be hidden within the texture of the crochet. Decorate the doily by stitching on a selection of beads and buttons.

3 Cut three pieces of yarn each 16 in. (40 cm) long and knot them together 4 in. (10 cm) from the top end. Below the knot, braid the three lengths together for 6 in. (15 cm) and then tie another knot to secure the braid. Repeat two more times to make three braids in total.

4 Gather the feathers together into three bunches, with about 4–5 feathers per bunch. Secure the bunches by winding an 8-in. (20-cm) length of sewing thread around the shafts of the feathers and tying it in a tight knot.

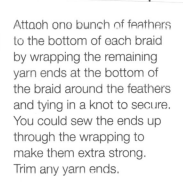

5 Attach one bunch of feathers to the bottom of each braid by wrapping the remaining yarn ends at the bottom of the braid around the feathers and tying in a knot to secure. You could sew the ends up through the wrapping to make them extra strong. Trim any yarn ends.

6 Space the braids out evenly along the bottom of the hoop. Stitch each braid in place using the 4-in. (10-cm) lengths of yarn left at the top of the braid. Trim off any excess yarn. Thread the ribbon through the top of the hoop and tie in a knot to make a hanging loop.

EYE MASK

This pretty eye mask will help you sleep as well as look glamorous at bedtime!

1 Photocopy and enlarge the eye mask template on page 116, then use it to cut out the shape once in each of the pink dotted fabric, pink fleece, and batting. Trim the batting mask shape down by ⅜ in. (1 cm) all the way around the edge.

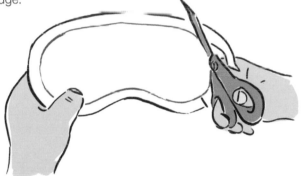

2 Prepare the ruffle by working a running stitch (see page 12) all the way along the length of the netting approx. ³⁄₁₆ in. (0.5 cm) in from one edge. Keep the needle attached to the thread and pull to gather the length of netting into a ruffle. Make a small stitch to hold the gathers in place.

Skill Level ✂

YOU WILL NEED

10 x 6 in. (25 x 15 cm) pink dotted fabric

10 x 6 in. (25 x 15 cm) pink fleece fabric

10 x 6 in. (25 x 15 cm) batting (wadding)

Scissors

60 x 2 in. (150 x 5 cm) strip of yellow netting

Sewing needle and thread

Pins

Sewing machine and thread (optional)

26 in. (65 cm) small pink rickrack braid

12 in. (30 cm) black elastic, or to fit head

12 in. (30 cm) narrow pink and white ribbon

10 in. (25 cm) pink lace ribbon

Small square rhinestone buckle

Short length of owl motif ribbon

Sequins

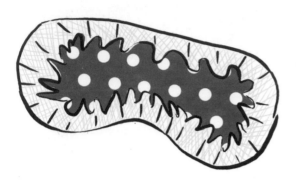

3 Pin and tack the ruffle around the edge on the right side of the pink dotted fabric mask shape, with the ruffle facing inward as shown in the diagram.

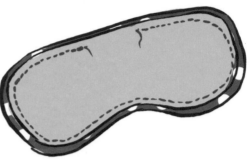

4 Place the fleece mask shape on top of the dotted fabric mask shape with right sides together. Stitch by hand or machine round the edge, using a ⅜-in. (1-cm) seam allowance. Leave a 2-in. (5-cm) gap at the top of the mask for turning. Trim the seams and then turn the mask right side out through the gap.

5 Insert the batting mask shape through the gap and move it around until it sits flat. Fold under the raw edges of the gap and pin. Pin the rickrack braid all the way around the edge of the dotted fabric and either hand stitch or machine zigzag over the top to keep it in place, which will close the gap at the same time. Stitch one end of the elastic to each side of the eye mask.

6 Fold a length of pink and white ribbon into a loop and then hand stitch the loop onto the top right-hand corner of the eye mask.

TIP
You can use any
motif ribbon to
thread onto the
buckle, or you can
replace the buckle
and ribbon with
a rhinestone pin
or a badge of
your choice.

7 Work running stitch along the bottom edge of
the lace ribbon and gather in the same way as
in Step 2, but this time pull as tight as possible
and tie a knot in both ends of the thread to
make a gathered flower. Stitch the flower onto
the eye mask over the ribbon loop. Thread the
owl motif ribbon onto the buckle and then stitch
the buckle on top of the flower. Sew the sequins
onto random dots.

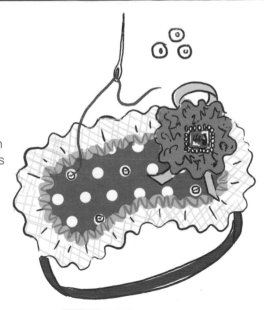

TUTTI FRUTTI CANDLES

Candles are easy to make, but be careful when working with the hot wax. Never leave burning candles unattended.

YOU WILL NEED

Colored sundae glass

Selection of candies

2 plastic straws

Sticky tape

4 plain long table candles

8 in. (20 cm) candle wick

Large saucepot with small pot that will fit inside

Tongs

Glass jug

Colored glass beads

Ribbon

1 Fill half the sundae glass with a selection of candies. Lower the wick into the glass to work out how long it should be—it needs to sit slightly above the sweets—then cut it to the correct length. Tape two straws together at each end, then insert the tip of the wick between them in the center. Place the wick into the sundae glass with the straws resting on the rim of the glass—this will stop the wick floating over to one side.

You may need some adult supervision for Steps 2 and 3.

2 Half fill the large saucepot with water, put onto the hob and bring to a boil. Place the table candles into the smaller pot and sit this on top of the large pot to create a bain marie. Leave the wax to heat until it turns liquid. Remove all the table candle wicks using the tongs.

3 Carefully pour the melted wax from the pan into a glass jug over the sink. Pour the wax from the jug to fill the sundae glass with wax to within ¾ in. (2 cm) of the top.

4 When the wax is almost solid at the top, carefully remove the straws making sure not to pull out the candle wick. Sprinkle a few colored glass beads onto the top of the candle for decoration.

5 When the wax is completely cold, tie a length of ribbon around the top of the sundae glass and tie into a neat bow. Trim the wick to ⅜ in. (1 cm).

MAGNETIC MAKEUP BOARD

Fed up of searching through your makeup bag for your lipgloss or blusher? This magnetic board provides a great way to keep all your makeup in sight and will look pretty on your wall, too.

Skill Level ✂ ✂ ✂

YOU WILL NEED

Magnetic bulletin board

Pliers

Old ornate picture frame

Tape measure or ruler

Fabric to fit frame

Scissors

Hot glue gun

Spray paint

Fine sandpaper

Flat magnets or self-adhesive magnetic strip

1 Using a pair of pliers, remove the old frame from the magnetic bulletin board, if it has one, so you just have a flat metal sheet. Measure your picture frame on the back from side to side and from top to bottom from the edges of the groove around the inside edge. Cut the metal sheet to fit into the back of the frame.

You may need some adult supervision for Steps 1, 2, 3, and 5.

2 Cut a piece of fabric to the same size as the metal sheet. Use the hot glue gun to stick the fabric to the metal sheet around the edges—pull the fabric gently as you stick so it is nice and flat.

3 In a well-ventilated room or outside, use the spray to paint the ornate picture frame. Put some old newsprint under the picture frame when you spray it to avoid getting paint everywhere. Leave it to dry completely.

4 Rub the frame lightly with the sandpaper over the top of the decoration to take away a little of the paint for a shabby chic effect. Use the hot glue gun to stick the metal sheet into the channel on the back of the picture frame.

5 Use the hot glue gun to attach a flat magnet to the back of each of your favorite make-up pots. If you have a self-adhesive magnet strip you can simply peel off the backing and stick a square onto each pot. For heavy items you may need to use two magnets.

COLLAGE COASTERS

Collaging is a great way to use up scrap pieces of paper and fabric. You can even cut out photos that you like from magazines to use on these coasters.

1 Cut out small pieces of patterned paper, scraps of tissue paper, pictures from magazines, and interesting bits of old sewing patterns. Play around with the pieces on a flat surface until you have made an attractive design.

2 Spread a thin and even covering of PVA glue over the surface of one of the tiles—don't leave any blobs of glue that might bleed through the paper. Stick down the papers and images to make your design on the tile. You will need a bit more glue if the design has several layers. Make up the other tiles in the same way.

3 Use the stamps and ink pad to stamp some random letters or images onto small pieces of colored or decorative paper. Cut out around the stamped areas and stick the pieces to the tiles with dabs of glue.

4 While the glue is still wet, scatter a few tiny nail art sequins and decorations across each tile. When the glue has dried enough so they won't move, brush another layer of glue over the top. Leave the tiles to dry completely.

5 Turn each tile over and spread a thin layer of glue across the back. Carefully stick a square of felt down on the back of the tile, making sure the edges line up. Turn the tiles over again and brush a layer of craft varnish over the surface to protect the images. Allow to dry completely before using your coasters.

BUNNY PENCIL CASE

This pencil case, shaped like a rabbit, is so easy to make! You only need basic sewing skills, fleece, and scraps of fabric.

Skill Level

YOU WILL NEED

10⅛ x 11 in. (26 x 28 cm)
of pink fleece

Tape measure

Scissors

Pins

10⅛ x 5½ in. (26 x 14 cm)
of Bondaweb

Small scraps of floral and
patterned fabric

Iron

Embroidery needle

White and pink embroidery floss

5 in. (12.5 cm) pink zipper

Sewing machine

Small amount of fiberfill
toy stuffing

6 in. (15 cm) narrow ribbon

You may need some adult supervision for Steps 2 and 3.

1 Cut the pink fleece into two pieces, each measuring 10½ x 5½ in. (26 x 14 cm). Place the two pieces one on top of one another and pin together. Photocopy and enlarge the rabbit template on page 116, then pin the paper shape onto the back of the fleece. Cut around the rabbit ears at the top.

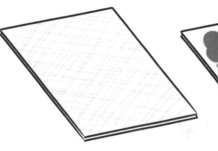

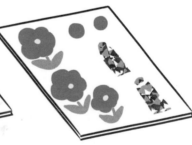

2 Place pieces of Bondaweb onto the wrong side of the floral and patterned fabric and iron in place following the directions on the Bondaweb packet. Cut out a few of the flower motifs and two ear shapes. Cut out two small circles for the cheeks.

3 Peel away the paper backing and place the flower, ears and cheeks onto one piece of the fleece using the photograph as a guide for position. Use an iron to fix these in place following the directions on the Bondaweb packet.

4 Using white embroidery floss, work back stitch around the flowers, cheeks, and ear pieces. Add two French knots for each eye. Embroider the nose and whiskers as shown. For instructions on how to do the stitches see pages 10–12.

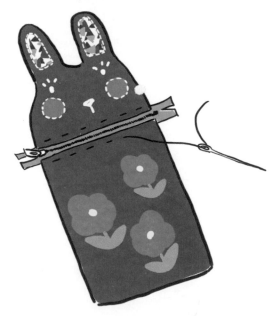

5 Leaving a gap of ⅜ in. (1 cm) under the nose embroidery, cut across the decorated piece of pink fleece to create a space for the zipper. Fold under the cut edges on both parts and pin the folds onto either side of the zipper. Baste (tack) the zipper in place.

6 Use a sewing machine to stitch the zipper securely in place and then remove the basting (tacking) stitches.

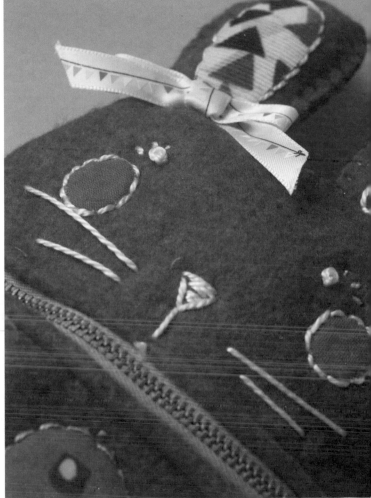

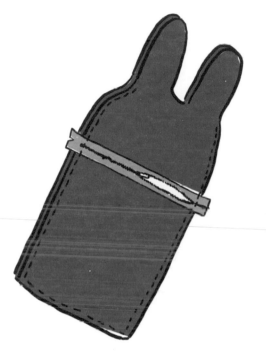

7 Place the front and back pieces with right sides together. Partly open the zipper. Pin and then machine stitch around the side edges with a ⅜-in. (1-cm) seam allowance, leaving the top open. Turn the case right side out through the top edge.

8 Using pink embroidery floss, sew blanket stitch around the top of the ears and across the top of the head to close the top of the case. Push a little stuffing into each ear and then sew small running stitches across the bottom of each ear to keep the stuffing in place. Make a small ribbon bow and stitch onto one of the ears as shown.

PRETTY SOAP

These soaps will look lovely in the bathroom or could be the perfect homemade gift for friends and relatives.

Skill Level ✂ ✂ ✂ ✂

YOU WILL NEED

Approx. 18 oz (500 g) clear soap base, cut into cubes

Jug

Plastic wrap (cling film)

Microwave

Drops of food coloring of choice

Drops of food essence of choice

Wooden spoon

Heart and flower silicon molds

1 Place the soap base cubes into a jug and cover with plastic wrap. Place into the microwave to melt for about two minutes in short bursts; be careful not to overcook—the soap just needs to heat up enough to melt, so check regularly and remove the jug as soon as the soap is all liquid.

2 Add a drop or two of the food coloring to the soap mix until it is the color you want. Add a drop of the food essence for scent. Stir gently but thoroughly.

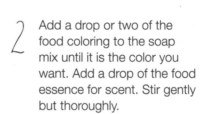

You may need some adult supervision for Steps 1 and 3.

TIPS

Clear soap base cubes can be bought from soap-making suppliers (see page 127). The amount you need will depend on the size of your molds.

For larger quantities, melt the soap base cubes in a pan on the hob. If a skin starts to form while you are adding the color and scent, this is just the soap setting, so just heat it up a little until it melts again.

3 Pour the mixture into the molds and leave to cool. When they are fully cool and hard, pop the soaps out of the silicon molds.

TIP
Why not try creating star- or
heart-shaped felt flowers? Simply
draw the shape you want and
use it as a template to cut out
the felt pieces.

POMPOM FLOWERS

Why buy real flowers when you can make these lovely pompom flowers that will last forever?

1. Color the skewers green with the paint or felt tip pen and allow to dry. Copy the flower template on page 119 and draw around it twice onto each sheet of felt. Cut out the flowers carefully and place to one side.

2. Cut 8 in. (20 cm) from the turquoise yarn and set aside. Take the metal fork and the remaining turquoise yarn and wrap the yarn around the fork prongs until you have used up the entire length.

3. Thread one end of the 8-in. (20-cm) length of turquoise yarn through the middle prong of the fork at the bottom. Tie the ends around the strands of yarn very tightly and knot in place.

4. Slide the yarn off the fork, wrap the ends of the tie around the middle again, and tie another knot. Slide the scissors through the loops of yarn on each side and cut to make a mini pompom. Fluff up the pompom and trim any ends to make a neat ball, but do not cut off the two long tie ends because they are needed to fix the pompom to the flower.

5 Repeat Steps 2–4 with the other yarn colors so you have five pompoms in total. Choose a pompom for each felt flower, mixing colors. Thread one end of a pompom tie into the embroidery needle and push through a felt flower slightly to one side of the center. Repeat with the other end.

6 Tie the ends tightly together on the back, inserting the end of a skewer into the knot. Trim the yarn ends if they are still quite long. Take the matching color felt flower and coat one side with a thin layer of PVA glue. Stick onto the back of the first flower to hide the fixing knot for a neat finish.

7 Thread the needle with a contrasting color of embroidery floss and oversew (see page 11) around the edges of the felt flower. Repeat until all your flowers are made, trim the skewers down if necessary and arrange in the vase.

FELT PENCIL TOPPERS

Jazz up your pens and pencils with these fun felt character toppers. They are so easy to make; just cut out the simple shapes and stitch together, then embellish with sequins, buttons, and bows.

1 Copy the templates on page 117 and mark 2 strawberries on the red felt, 1 leaf and 2 doll bodies on the lime green felt, 1 doll shawl on the dark red felt, 1 doll apron on the gray felt, 1 doll face on the cream felt, 2 owl bodies on the turquoise felt, and two owl wings on the coral felt. Cut out the felt shapes.

2 To make the strawberry, oversew the leaf onto the top of one of the strawberries as shown, using green embroidery floss. Sew the sequins onto the strawberry using yellow floss. Place the second strawberry onto the back of the decorated one and sew the two layers together with red floss using blanket stitch (see page 11), leaving a gap at the bottom.

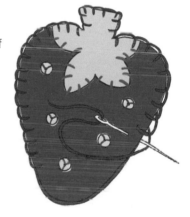

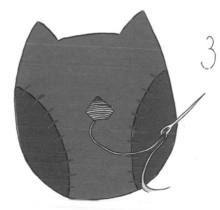

3 To make the owl, oversew the wings on either side of one owl body using turquoise floss, as shown. Embroider a diamond shape in satin stitch (see page 11) in the center for the beak. Sew on the button eyes on either side of the beak (see page 12).

4 Tie the ribbon into a bow, trim to size and stitch onto the owl's chest. Place the second owl body onto the back of the decorated one and sew together with coral floss using blanket stitch, leaving a gap at the bottom.

5 To make the Russian doll, oversew the shawl to the top of the doll body using green floss as shown. Place the face shape onto the shawl at the top and stitch eyes and a smile in burgundy floss to keep it in place, using the photograph opposite as a guide.

6 Place the apron and large sequin on the lower part of the doll and stitch through the sequin with coral floss to attach both the apron and sequin to the doll. Place the second doll body on the back of the decorated one and sew together with lime green floss using blanket stitch, leaving a gap at the bottom.

7 Slip the toppers onto the ends of your pencils through the gaps left unstitched at the bottom of each one.

CHAPTER 2
CLOTHES AND ACCESSORIES

This section features a great range of different crafting techniques—there is certainly something for everyone! There are lots of trendy ideas like the tie-dye T-shirt and shrink plastic jewelry, as well as simple yet effective ways to upcycle your old shoes, clothes, and jewelry. If you want to develop your knitting skills further then you'll find some great projects in this chapter—have a go at the knitted panda slippers, they are just so cute!

KNITTED HEADBAND

This design has been knitted in a straight line of moss stitch so it's perfect for beginner knitters. The pretty I-cord flower gives it a "girly-girl" appeal.

1. Knit the headband following the pattern below.

2. Coil up the I-cord to make 5 petals and pin to hold in place. Sew through bottom edge of each petal to create flower shape.

3. To make the bobble cast on one stitch using C and US size 10½ (6.5 mm) double pointed needles, which you work into three times to make three stitches: knit into the cast-on stitch but do not complete the stitch, carry the yarn forward in between the needles, purl into the cast-on stitch but do not complete the stitch, carry the yarn back between the needles, knit into the cast-on stitch and complete the stitch.

KNITTING PATTERN

Gauge (Tension)

8 sts and 11 rows over 4 in. (10 cm) square of stockinette (stocking) stitch using US size 17 (12 mm) needles.

Pattern

Cast on 8 sts using B and US size 17 (12 mm) needles.

Row 1: K1, *p1, k1; rep from * to last st, p1.

Row 2: P1, *k1, p1; rep from * to last st, k1.

Rep Rows 1 and 2 until work measures 20 in. (50 cm).

Bind (cast) off.

I-cord flower

Cast on 2 sts using A and US size 10½ (6.5 mm) double pointed needles. Work an I-cord (see page 56) 20 in. (50 cm) long.

Making up

Fold the headband right sides together and join the ends using mattress stitch (see step 2, page 61). Turn right side out.

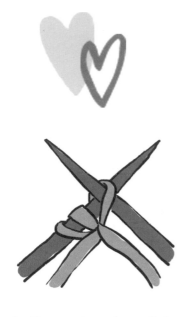

4 You now have three stitches on the needle. Turn the knitting round so that wrong side is facing and purl the three stitches as normal. Turn the knitting round again and knit the three stitches.

5 Turn the knitting round again and purl two stitches together, purl the last stitch.

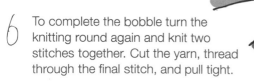

6 To complete the bobble turn the knitting round again and knit two stitches together. Cut the yarn, thread through the final stitch, and pull tight.

7 Position the bobble onto the center of the I-cord flower and attach with the yarn end using an overstitch.

8 Attach the flower to one side of the headband using an overstitch.

KNITTED MITTENS

These sweet pink mitts will keep your hands cozy! They have been knitted in a simple rib and stockinette stitch using pure new wool, and decorated with fluffy pompoms and sparkly beads.

YOU WILL NEED

Skill Level ✂✂

SMC Wash and Filz It!

• 2 x 1¾ oz (50 g) balls (109 yd/100 m) of Pink 00011 (A)

• 1 x 1¾ oz (50 g) ball (55 yd/50 m) of White 00002 (B)

US size 10½ (6.5 mm) knitting needles

Set of four US size 8 (5 mm) double pointed needles

Stitch holder

Darning needle

Scissors

1/16 in. (3 mm) pink glass beads

Sewing needle and pink sewing thread

Cardstock

Size: One size

Knit a pair of mittens following the pattern below.

KNITTING PATTERN

Gauge (Tension)

13 sts and 19 rows over 4 in. (10 cm) square of stockinette (stocking) stitch using US size 10½ (6.5 mm) needles.

Pattern

LEFT MITTEN

Cast on 28 sts using US size 10½ (6.5 mm) needles and A.

Row 1 (RS): *K1, p1; rep from * to end.

Rows 2–8: Rep Row 1.

Rows 9–16: Work in stockinette (stocking) stitch.

Row 17: K4, break yarn, place next 4 sts onto stitch holder for thumb, join in new yarn and knit to last 20 sts.

Row 18: P20, turn work and cast on 4 sts, turn work, purl to end.

Rows 19–34: Work in stockinette (stocking) stitch.

Row 35: K1, *k2tog, k1; rep from * to end.

Row 36: Purl.

Row 37: Knit.

Row 38: Purl.

Row 39: K1, k2tog across row.

Break yarn and thread through remaining stitches.

THUMB:
Knit 2 sts from stitch holder onto needle 1. Knit rem 2 sts from stitch holder onto needle 2 and pick up and knit 1 st from side edge (3 sts on needle 2). Pick up and knit 4 sts from cast-on edge onto needle 3 and pick up and knit 1 st from side edge. (5 sts on needle 3)

Knit in the round for 8 rounds.

Cut yarn and thread through rem stitches, pull up tightly and secure.

RIGHT MITTEN

Rows 1–16: Work as Left mitten.

Row 17: K20, break yarn, place 4 sts onto stitch holder for thumb), join in new yarn and knit last 4 sts.

Row 18: P4, turn work and cast on 4 sts, turn work, purl to end.

Rows 19–39: Work as for Left mitten to end.

THUMB:
Work as for Left mitten.

Making up

Fold over ribbed lower edge of each mitten and with RS facing sew up using mattress stitch (see step 2, page 61).

2 Sew small beads to front of each mitten using the photograph on page 55 as a guide.

3 To make the I-cord cast on three stitches using B and US size 8 (5 mm) double pointed needles. Knit the three stitches from the left-hand needle onto the right-hand needle as normal.

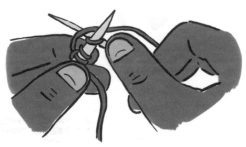

4 Now slide all the stitches just worked to the right end of the right-hand needle, and move this needle over to your left hand so you can start knitting again from the right end of the needle.

5 With the yarn at the back of the knitting, insert the (empty) right needle into the first stitch on the left needle, pull the yarn tightly along the back of the knitting and knit the stitch. Then knit the other two stitches. Keep repeating Steps 4 and 5 until the I-cord measures 14 in. (35 cm).

6 Make four pompoms with a diameter of 2 in. (5 cm) using B (see page 59 for how to make a pompom). Tie both I-cords into a bow shape and attach a pompom to each end using an overstitch.

7 Position the bows onto the mittens using the photograph on page 55 as a guide and attach using an overstitch.

SLIPPER SOCKS

These super cute panda slippers are sure to put a smile on your sleepy face in the morning or at bedtime! They are really straightforward to make, knitted using super-chunky and soft merino wool and embellished with lots of fun details.

Knit two slipper socks following the pattern below. The knitting pattern shows different numbers in some places for the different sizes, in the order small(**medium**:large). It can be a good idea to go through the pattern before you start knitting and highlight the figures for the size you are making.

Skill Level ✄✄

YOU WILL NEED

Rowan Big Wool

- 1:1:2 x 3½ oz (100 g) balls (87:**87**:174 yd/80:**80**:160 m) of White Hot 001

US size 11 (8 mm) knitting needles

Cardstock

Scissors

1 square each of black and white felt

4 small black buttons, ⁵⁄₁₆ in. (8 mm) diameter

Sewing needle

White sewing thread

Fabric glue

Small amount of black wool yarn

Darning needle

Oddment of pink wool yarn

Sizes:
Small (to fit sizes US 2–3/UK 1–2)

Medium (to fit sizes US 4–6/UK 3–5)

Large (to fit sizes US 7–10/UK 6–9)

KNITTING PATTERN

Gauge (Tension)

10 sts and 15 rows over 4 in. (10 cm) square of stockinette (stocking) stitch using US size 11 (8 mm) needles.

Pattern

(make 2 the same)

Cast on 24(**26**:28) sts using white yarn.

Row 1: K9, p6(**8**:10), k9.

Row 2 (RS): Knit.

Rows 3–20: Rep rows 1–2 nine more times.

SHAPE TOE:
Work in stockinette (stocking) stitch for 9(**15**:19) rows starting with a purl row and ending with a purl row.

Next row: K2tog to end. (12(**13**:14 sts)

Next row: Purl.

SMALL AND LARGE SIZES ONLY:
Next row: K2tog to end. (6:7 sts)

MEDIUM SIZE ONLY:
Next row: K2tog to last st, k1. (**7** sts)

ALL SIZES:
Cut yarn leaving a 4¾ in. (12 cm) tail and draw through remaining sts, gather up, and secure.

Making up

Fold the slipper socks in half and sew up along the cast-on edge, pulling in the heel section slightly to curve the heel.

Sew up toe section using mattress stitch (see step 2, page 61) until you reach the beginning of the stockinette (stocking) stitch.

2 Copy the templates on page 117 onto cardstock and cut them out. Using the templates, cut four outer eyes and two heart noses from black felt, and four inner eyes from white felt.

3 Place an inner eye onto the center of an outer eye and use the sewing needle and white thread to stitch a button on top to hold the two layers together. Repeat for the other eyes to make one pair of eyes for each slipper.

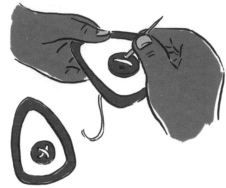

4 Using the photograph opposite as a guide, attach the eyes and nose to the toe section of each slipper sock using a little fabric glue. Using black wool, work in back stitch (see page 11) to create the mouth. Using an oddment of pink wool, work blanket stitch (see page 11) around the opening for the foot.

5 Cut two circles of cardstock each 2 in. (5 cm) in diameter. Cut a hole out of the center of both circles to make two rings and then stack the two rings together. Wrap black wool through the center hole and all around the outer edge until the center hole is filled with yarn.

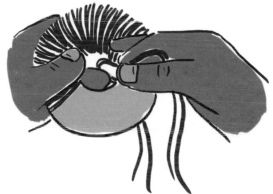

6 Cut the loops around the outer edge of the cardstock rings and ease them apart—don't take them off completely yet. Tie a length of black yarn between the cardstock rings, pull very tight, and make a double knot. Remove the cardstock rings and fluff the pompom up, trimming any long ends. Make three more pompoms and stitch two to the top of each slipper sock.

KNITTED SNOOD

This is a great project for a beginner knitter, designed using four simple stitches. It has been made with chunky pure wool so will take no time at all to knit, and will feel lovely and soft around your neck!

YOU WILL NEED

SMC Wash and Filz It! Big

- 2 x 3½ oz (100 g) balls (109 yd/100 m) of Petrol 00307 (A)
- 1 x 3½ oz (100 g) ball (55 yd/50 m) of Pflaume 00326 (B)
- 1 x 3½ oz (100 g) ball (55 yd/50 m) of Steel 00321 (C)

Skill Level ✂ ✂

US size 17 (12 mm) knitting needles

Darning needle

Scissors

Size: One size

Knit the two halves of the snood following the pattern below. Place the two pieces with right sides facing up and with the two edges to be joined next to one another.

KNITTING PATTERN

Gauge (Tension)

8 sts and 11 rows over 4 in. (10 cm) square of stockinette (stocking) stitch using US size 17 (12 mm) needles.

How to make a bobble (MB)

Working into next st k1, p1, and k1. Turn work and purl 3 sts. Turn work and knit 3 sts. Turn work and p2tog, p1. Turn work and k2tog.

Pattern

(make 2)

Cast on 34 sts using yarn A and US size 17 (12 mm) needles.

Row 1 (RS): K2, *p2, k2; rep from * to end.

Row 2: P2, *k2, p2; rep from * to end.

Rows 3–6: Rep Rows 1 and 2 two more times.

Row 7: Change to B and knit across row.

Row 8: Purl.

Row 9: Change to A and knit across row.

Row 10: Purl.

Row 11: Change to C and knit across row.

Row 12: Purl.

Row 13: K4, *MB, k4; rep from * to end.

Row 14: Purl.

Row 15: Knit.

Row 16: Purl.

Row 17: Change to B, knit across row.

Row 18: *K1, p1; rep from * to end.

Row 19: *P1, k1; rep from * to end.

Row 20: *K1, p1; rep from * to end.

Row 21: Change to A and knit across row.

Row 22: Change to C and purl across row.

Row 23: Change to B and knit across row.

Row 24: Change to A and purl across row.

Rows 25–30: Rep Rows 1 and 2 three times.

Bind (cast) off.

Making up

Darn in all ends neatly.

2 Thread a darning needle with a length of yarn and pick up the first two horizontal bars between the first and the second stitches on the left piece. Take the needle across to the right piece and pick up the first two bars on that piece. Go back across to the left piece and pick up the next two bars between the stitches and then across to pick up the same two bars on the opposite piece. Continue like this, firmly pulling the yarn as you go to bring the two pieces together

3 Sew the other seam in the same way to finish the snood. Use the darning needle to weave in any long ends of yarn to neaten up the knitting.

CLOTHES AND ACCESSORIES

DECORATED SNEAKERS

If you have a plain, boring pair of old or new sneakers, why not transform them with this simple stamp and fabric paint technique? We've used bows here, but you could try other motifs for a different look.

Skill Level ✂ ✂ ✂

YOU WILL NEED

Bow outline stamp and ink pad

Pair of canvas sneakers

Fine to medium paintbrush

Fabric paints in red, bright pink, and white

Black fine liner fabric pen

Hot-fix rhinestones and an iron, or plain rhinestones and a hot glue gun

64 in. (160 cm) of coordinating grosgrain ribbon

1 Remove the shoelaces from the sneakers and set aside. Apply an even coating of ink onto the stamp; you could either use the paintbrush for this or press the stamp carefully onto the ink pad. Stamp the bow motif over both shoes in a random design. Let the ink dry.

2 Using the paintbrush, fill in the bow motifs with red fabric paint. When the red is dry, use the paintbrush to blend a little of the bright pink and white fabric paints onto the bow design to create a more three-dimensional effect, following the photograph as a guide.

3 When all the fabric paint is completely dry, carefully outline each bow motif using the black fine liner pen. You can also use the fine liner to add any extra details to the bow design.

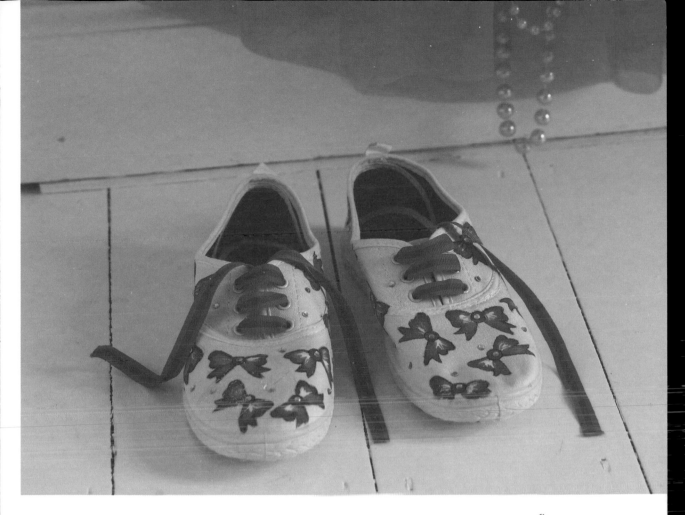

4 If using hot-fix rhinestones, place them at random on each shoe. Following the instructions on the packet, hold a hot iron over each rhinestone to melt the glue on the back and fix it in place. Apply plain rhinestones by using a dab of glue from a hot glue gun.

You may need some adult supervision for Step 4

5 Cut the coordinating ribbon into two pieces, each the same length as the shoelaces. Thread the ribbon through the eyelet holes on each sneaker to use as laces.

OWL FLEECE TOTE

This adorable bag is just the thing to brighten up your day! It has been made using colorful fleece fabric, felts, and old denims. For added style, you also have the option of adding a patterned lining. It's perfect for carrying all of your bits and bobs around with you!

Skill Level ✂✂

YOU WILL NEED

Thin cardstock

Marker pen

Scissors

40 in. (1 m) square pink fleece fabric

Fabric scissors

Small squares of fuchsia and mustard yellow felt

Piece of denim from on old pair of jeans, skirt or shirt

Extra strong fabric glue

1½-in. (4-cm) wide strip of iron-on Vilene interfacing

Iron

Pins

Sewing machine

Pink sewing thread

Tape measure

40 in. (1 m) square patterned fabric for lining (optional)

Size: One size

1 Photocopy and enlarge the template for the main bag on page 119. Use the template to draw a pattern piece for the front and back of the bag onto the cardstock and cut out. Place the pattern onto the wrong side of the pink fleece fabric, draw around it twice, and cut the shapes out.

2 Copy the templates on page 118 and use them for the features as follows: for the owl face, trace a pair of outer eyes and the longest feather strip onto the fuchsia felt. Trace the beak, smallest feather strip, wings, and a pair of second size shaped eyes onto the mustard yellow felt. Trace a pair of third size eyes and the middle size feather strip onto the back of the fleece fabric. Trace a pair of inner eyes onto a corner of the denim. Cut all the shapes out.

3 Take a set of the eye pieces and stick the layers together with a little fabric glue to make up the eye, following the photograph opposite as a guide. Repeat to make up the second eye. Take the front piece of the bag and position the eyes, beak, feathers, and wings on the right side of the fabric, following the photograph as a guide. Attach the pieces using fabric glue.

4 Iron the strip of Vilene interfacing on the wrong side of the fleece across the top of the front and back bag pieces. Fold the top of each piece over by 1½ in. (4 cm) and pin. Stitch along the bottom edge of the hem to hold it in place using a sewing machine.

You may need some adult supervision for Step 4.

5 For the denim handles, cut two 25 x 3¼ in. (62 x 8 cm) strips of denim. Fold the strips in half lengthwise with right sides together. Stitch the long edges using a sewing machine. Turn the handles right side out and press with the iron.

6 Position the ends of one handle on the wrong side of the front of the bag at the top and about 2 in. (5 cm) in from each side. Pin in place. Stitch a box shape on each handle end with the sewing machine and then add a diagonal line in both directions. Repeat to add the other handle to the back of the bag.

7 Place the front and back of the bag right sides together. Stitch around the sides and bottom ⅜ in. (1 cm) in from the edge using the sewing machine. Turn the bag right side out.

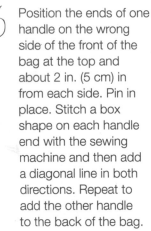

8 Using the cardstock bag pattern again, cut a front and back piece from the lining fabric. Place the lining pieces right sides together and stitch around the sides and bottom ⅜ in. (1 cm) in from the edge using the sewing machine. Fold the top of the bag lining over to the outside by 1½ in. (4 cm) and press.

9 Push the lining inside the bag with wrong sides together and make sure it lies flat. Pin around the top edge of the bag to hold the lining in place and then stitch round using the sewing machine.

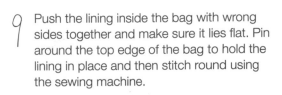

SHRINK PLASTIC JEWELRY

This fantastic and innovative craft technique is a great way to create personalized jewelry using your own doodles, drawings, stamps, and photographs.

Skill Level ✂ ✂ ✂ ✂

YOU WILL NEED

Computer and printer or stamp and ink pad

2–3 sheets of shrink plastic

Pencil crayons, paints and inks (optional)

Scissors

Hole punch

Baking tray

Oven

Nylon beading thread and needle

Assorted small beads

52 in. (1.3 m) of narrow silk ribbon

Lip balm tube or similar (optional)

1 Select and save approx. 14 images of your choice into digital documents (remember that the image will shrink down to about a third of the original image size so bear that in mind when you change the size of your images). Print the images out onto a shrink plastic sheet.

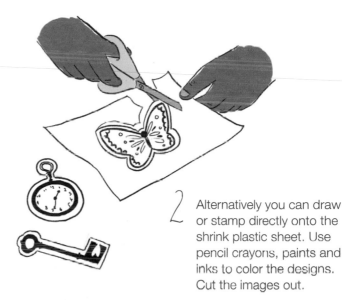

2 Alternatively you can draw or stamp directly onto the shrink plastic sheet. Use pencil crayons, paints and inks to color the designs. Cut the images out.

3 Use a hole punch to punch a hole in each shape just below the top edge, so it can be threaded onto the necklace.

4 Place the cut shapes on a baking tray and put into the oven following the manufacturer's instructions. Watch as the plastic heats up, shrivels up and then shrinks into a hard flat piece of plastic. Take the plastic charms out of the oven and leave to cool.

You may need some adult supervision for Steps 4 and 8.

5 Using a needle and nylon beading thread, construct the necklace by threading the plastic charms on with several beads between each one. Make sure that the last bead on each side is fairly large, loop through it, and tie it off to secure all the beads and charms in place.

6 Cut two 6 in. (15 cm) lengths of silk ribbon and then cut the remaining ribbon in half. Thread a long length through the last bead at each end of the necklace until the bead is at the center of the ribbon and then knot the ribbon to secure. Tie the two short lengths of ribbon into small bows over the join on each side.

7   For the ring, cut a piece of shrink plastic approx. 5¼ x 1¼ in. (13 x 3 cm). Stamp or draw your designs onto the strip of plastic and put it into the oven as explained in Step 4.

8   When the plastic has shrunk, quickly take it out of the oven using oven gloves and before it completely cools bend it around a small tube (a lip balm stick is a good size). As the plastic cools and hardens it will keep the ring shape.

FELT IPOD AND CELLPHONE COZY

Needle felting is such a fun craft—it's super quick, easy to master, and doesn't require much skill. By using this technique you can create simple appliques without using fabric.

CUPCAKE DESIGN

1 Copy the phone and cupcake templates on page 119 onto cardstock and cut out. Use the phone template to cut two pieces from the felt square for the front and back of the cozy. Place the cupcake template onto one (front) felt piece and draw around it using a fabric marker pen to make an outline on the felt ready for needle felting.

2 Unravel small tufts of turquoise wool tops to create loose wispy pieces. Place the front felt piece onto the felting sponge. Holding the felting needle upright, start to punch the wisps of wool into the front felt piece inside the base of the cupcake outline. Continue to add thin, loose layers of wool tops until you have completely filled in the design. Repeat with white wool tops for the cupcake icing.

Skill Level ✂ ✂

YOU WILL NEED

Pencil

Cardstock

Scissors

Fabric marker pen

Felting sponge

Felting needle

Sewing needle

Green embroidery floss

Cupcake design

Fuchsia felt square

1 oz (25 g) ball of wool tops in each of turquoise, white, and pink

Packet of 6 mm gold bugle beads

White sewing thread

Bow design

Mustard yellow felt square

1 oz (25 g) ball of wool tops in turquoise and pink

Purple sequins

Purple sewing thread

3 Using the green embroidery floss, work lines of back stitch (see page 11) onto the base of the cupcake case using the photograph on page 71 as a guide. Using a sewing needle and a doubled length of white thread, stitch gold bugle beads to the icing part of the design.

You may need some adult supervision for Steps 2, 4, and 5.

4 Take a few thin tufts of pink wool top and twist together. Place round the outline of the base of the cupcake and punch with the felting needle. To neaten up the outline, angle the felting needle and punch along the sides of the design.

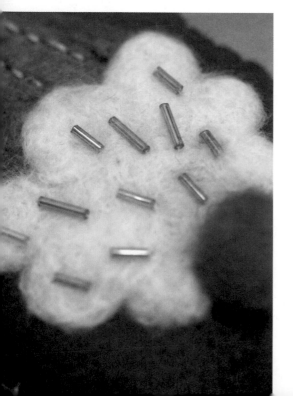

5 For the ¾-in. (2-cm) diameter three-dimensional pink cherry, wrap small tufts of pink wool tops around your index finger to create a rough ball shape. Put this onto the felting sponge and repeatedly punch with the felting needle, rotating the ball often. Keep wrapping thin layers of pink tops around the ball and punching with the needle until the ball is solid and the correct size. Attach the cherry to the top of the cupcake by punching through it with the felting needle.

6 Place the front and back felt pieces with wrong sides together and work blanket stitch (see page 11) around the sides and bottom of the cozy to hold the layers together, using green embroidery floss.

BOW DESIGN

Follow the steps for the cupcake cozy using the yellow mustard felt and the bow template on page 119. In Step 3, stitch the bow detail with green floss and the sequins with purple thread.

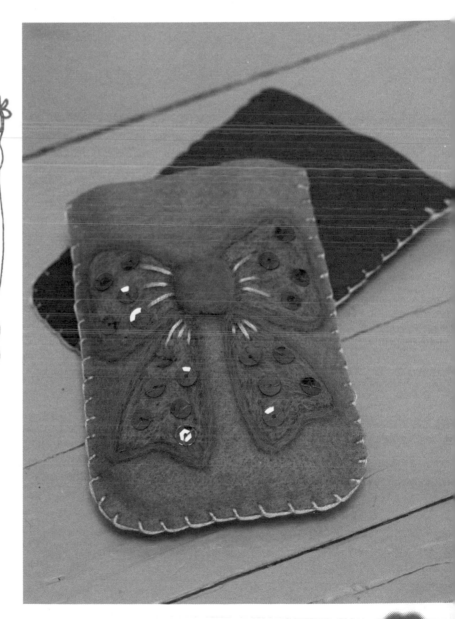

NOTEBOOK

Every girl needs a place to keep lists, make plans, and, most importantly, write her secrets. Why not create this cute notebook? The simple button and ribbon loop tie will keep all those prying eyes out!

Skill Level ✂ ✂

YOU WILL NEED

Color photocopier

Glue stick or double-sided tape

Thin white cardstock

Craft knife and cutting mat

Needle and thread

Sequins

Button

Short length of narrow ribbon

Adhesive tape

14 sheets of white copy paper

Long, heavy-duty stapler

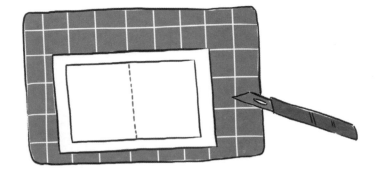

1 Color photocopy and enlarge the cover and inside cover notebook templates on page 121. Using a glue stick or double-sided tape, stick the cover to one side of the piece of white cardstock. Carefully using the craft knife and cutting mat, cut around the outside edge of the notebook cover template.

2 Thread the needle with matching thread and sew a few sequins to the cover of your notebook using the photograph opposite as a guide. Sew a medium-sized button in the center, just inside the outside edge as shown.

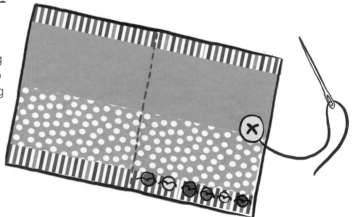

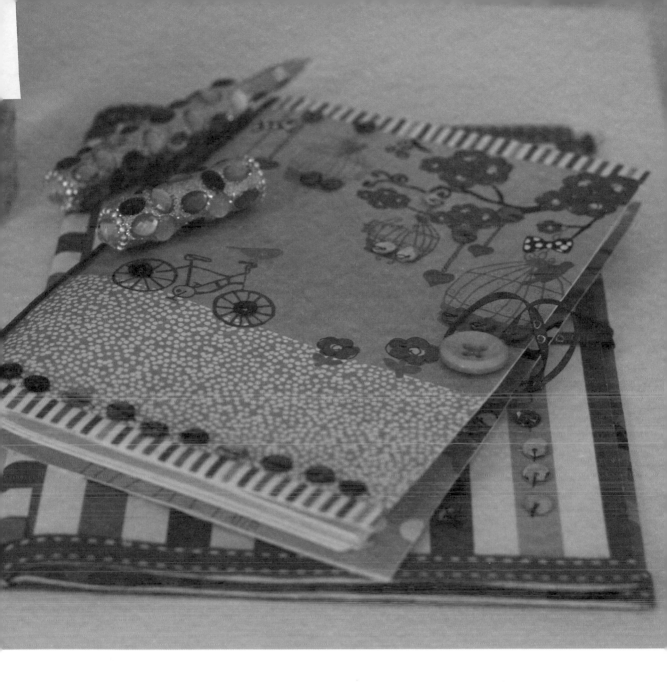

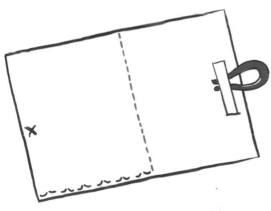

3 Turn the notebook cover over. Create a small loop with the ribbon. Stick the ends of the ribbon on the opposite side to the button, using adhesive tape, with the loop over the edge as shown. This ribbon loop will catch over the button to keep your notebook shut.

4 Using the glue stick or double-sided tape, carefully stick the inside cover to the reverse of the front cover and then carefully trim around the outside edge if necessary. The inside cover will hide all the stitching thread and make the notebook look much neater.

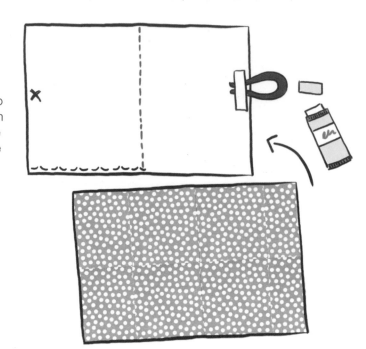

5 Cut down the sheets of white copy paper carefully, using the craft knife and cutting board, so they will fit inside the notebook cover. Fold all the sheets in half, crease, and then unfold.

6 Carefully fold the notebook cover in half. Place the white paper inside the notebook cover so all the center folds are in line. Turn the notebook over.

You may need some adult supervision for Steps 1 and 7.

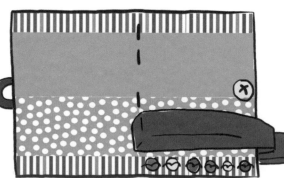

7 Using the long stapler, staple the cover and pages together. You may want to put the cutting mat underneath the stapler because you may have to apply lots of pressure to push the staples through all the layers.

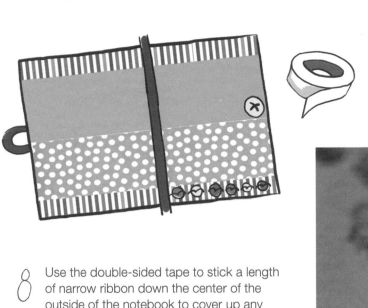

8 Use the double-sided tape to stick a length of narrow ribbon down the center of the outside of the notebook to cover up any unsightly staples. Fold the notebook closed and add the ribbon loop around the button.

COIN PURSE

Old zippers are perfect for making decorations: they look fantastic coiled up or looped into flowers, and can be added onto purses and bags as a fab accessory.

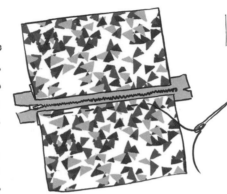

Skill Level ✂ ✂

YOU WILL NEED

4¾ x 12 in. (12 x 30 cm) piece of fabric

Tape measure

Scissors

Iron

Pins

Approx. 4¾ in. (12 cm) zipper

Sewing needle

Sewing thread

Sewing machine

4¾ x 12 in. (12 x 30 cm) piece of felt or fleece

Long metal zipper in a coordinating color

Hot glue gun (optional)

1 Cut the fabric into two pieces, each 4¾ x 6 in. (12 x 15 cm). Fold over to the wrong side by ⅜ in. (1 cm) along one long edge of each piece and finger press the fold. Pin the folded edge of each piece onto the smaller zipper, baste (tack) in place, and remove the pins. Using a zipper foot on the sewing machine, stitch down both sides of the zipper. Remove the basting stitches.

2 Half open the zipper and place the two fabric pieces right sides together. Machine stitch around the sides and bottom of the purse. Trim the seams. Open the zipper fully and turn the purse right sides out.

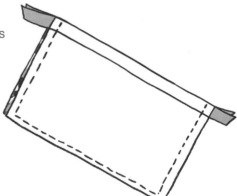

3 Cut the felt or fleece into two pieces, each 4¾ x 6 in. (12 x 15 cm). Place the pieces right sides together and stitch around the sides and bottom edge with a ⅝ in. (1.5 cm) seam allowance. Trim the seams. Push the lining inside the purse with wrong sides together. Fold over the top edge of the lining and neatly stitch the folded edge along the inside of the zipper.

4 To make the zipper flowers, unzip the long metal zipper and cut near the end to separate the two sides. Hold one end in your left hand and loop the zipper around to make the first petal. Make a small stitch through the center of the zipper flower to hold the loop in place.

5 Repeat to make five petals. Coil the remaining length of the zipper up to make a center for the flower and sew this in place.

6 Make the little rose buds by coiling up smaller lengths of zipper and stitching in place. When all the flowers are complete either sew them onto the purse or use a hot glue gun to attach them.

You may need some adult supervision for Step 6.

NAIL POLISH JEWELRY

Nail polish is a brilliant way to jazz up old or boring jewelry. Bright colors like these ones create bold statement pieces, while pastels give a delicate look, although you may need to paint an extra coat.

Skill Level ✂

YOU WILL NEED

Inexpensive rhinestone necklace

Pair of inexpensive rhinestone earrings

Inexpensive rhinestone bracelet

Nail polish in lilac, lemon, coral, and orange

Nail art decorations and sequins, if desired

1 Decide which rhinestones in each piece of jewelry you are going to paint and which color to use. Carefully paint each jewel with the chosen nail polish. If the jewels are large they may need a few coats.

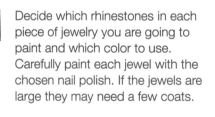

2 Decorate the items further by placing nail art decorations or sequins onto the nail polish whilst it is still wet. Allow the polish to dry completely before wearing the jewelry.

TIPS

Thrift stores and yard sales are good hunting grounds for old costume jewelry. Painting the jewels with nail polish is a great way to make odd pieces into a matching set.

If the nail polish starts becoming too thick and sticky as you work, add a couple of drops of nail polish remover and mix well.

If you make a mistake, carefully remove the polish using a drop of nail polish remover on a cotton swab tip.

FABRIC NECKLACE

Don't spend a fortune on store-bought fabric necklaces—simply use an old string of beads and a length of fabric to make a gorgeous piece of jewelry. They're also great to give as gifts!

Skill Level ✂✂

YOU WILL NEED

Approx. 40 x 4 in. (100 x 10 cm) strip of fabric

Needle and thread

Old key charm

Old chunky bead necklace or packet of wooden beads

40 in. (1 m) of coordinating ribbon

Hot glue gun

1 Fold the fabric in half lengthwise and stitch near to the long raw edges to make a tube. Turn the tube right side out.

2 Thread the key charm onto the fabric until it reaches the center. Tie the fabric into a knot to hold the charm in place.

3 Insert a bead into one end of the fabric tube and push it right down to the key charm. Tie a knot tightly in the fabric after the bead. Repeat this step until you have inserted five or six beads into one side. Now repeat on the other side of the tube to make the two sides of the necklace even. Knot the fabric at both ends then trim off any excess fabric.

TIPS

The strip of fabric will become shorter as a necklace because the knots use up some of the length. Adjust the length of the starting strip to get the length necklace you want—it's better to begin with a longer strip and cut the ends down later than to find the necklace is too short.

The fabric needs to be quite smooth and thick—silk is great.

You may need some adult supervision for Step 4.

4 Cut the length of ribbon into four equal pieces. Use a hot glue gun to stick one length of ribbon to the front and back of each end of the beaded necklace over the knot. When the glue is dry, tie a knot in the necklace at each end to cover where the ribbon meets the fabric.

TIP

The folded circles can be arranged onto the shoe in any way that you like. Here they are arranged around the front of the shoe in a semi-circular pattern, but they also look great as a full circular shape.

FLOWER PUMPS

Follow these simple steps to reinvent a pair of plain old pumps by making pretty fabric embellishments for them.

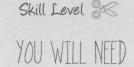

1 Using a compass, draw and cut a 2⅜-in. (6-cm) diameter circle template from cardstock. Draw around the template 20 times onto the wrong side of the fabric. Cut out all the circles.

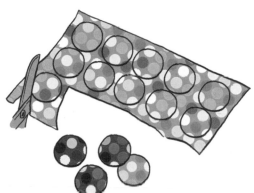

2 Fold the first fabric circle in half and then into quarters, with the patterned side on the outside. Make a couple of small stitches along the edge to hold the folds in place. Repeat this step with all the circles to make 20 petals.

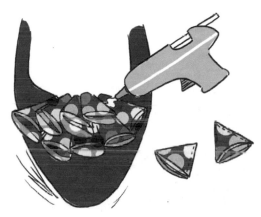

You may need some adult supervision for Steps 3 and 4.

3 Using the hot glue gun stick five of the petals around the curve of the front of the shoe—make sure each petal slightly overlaps the one before to make the flower look full.

4 Repeat Step 3 with the remaining five petals on top of the first layer. Fluff up the petals to create a full flower on the shoe. Repeat for the other shoe.

TIE-DYE TOP

Here's a blast from the past! Tie-dye is very on-trend again and so simple to do—try it out on a plain T-shirt or tank top and create your own unique design.

Skill Level

YOU WILL NEED

White 100% cotton top or T-shirt

Rubber bands

Rubber gloves

Pink cold water powder dye

Measuring jug

Glass jars

1 Scrunch up a handful of the top and twist a rubber band very tightly around the fabric—wherever you tie the band the fabric will not absorb the dye so will remain white. Repeat this all over the top in random places.

You may need some adult supervision for Steps 2 and 3.

2 Put on the rubber gloves and mix the powder dye with water in the measuring jug, following the manufacturer's instructions. Pour the mixed dye into glass jars—you can keep any unused dye for another project.

TIP
Create a multicolor
effect by using two or
more color dyes.
Simply dip different
sections of the top
into each color.

3 Work over a metal sink or spread a surface outside with lots of newsprint. Dip the tied areas of the fabric into the dye. Pour the dye over any remaining white areas, making sure it has covered the entire top.

4 Leave the top to absorb the dye for 30 minutes, or for as long as given in the dye instructions. Rinse out the top until the water runs clear. Remove all the rubber bands to reveal your tie-dye design and hang up to dry.

STAMPS AND STAMPED BAG

Make your very own stamps from a plain eraser! Go crazy and personalize purses, bags, cards, envelopes, gift tags, and lots more!

Skill Level

YOU WILL NEED

For the stamps

Tracing paper and pencil

8 erasers in various sizes

Craft knife

Ink pad (optional)

For the bag

16 x 32 in. (40 x 80 cm) pink fabric

Tape measure

Scissors

Light pink paint

Paintbrush

Sparkly nail varnish

Selection of buttons and sequins

Sewing needle and thread

Pins

12 in. (30 cm) decorative trimming

Sewing machine

Large fabric-covered button

1 Trace over one of the stamp design templates on page 117. Place the tracing paper face down onto the eraser and scribble over the back to transfer the outline of the design.

2 Carefully cut around the outline with the craft knife and then cut away the surface of the eraser around the design. Check your progress by stamping into an ink pad and then printing onto paper—if you can see any marks other than the design continue to cut away until you get a nice clean print. Repeat Steps 1–2 to make a selection of different stamps.

You may need some adult supervision for Step 2.

3 Cut the fabric into two pieces 16 x 12 in. (40 x 30 cm) and two strips 12 x 4 in. (30 x 10 cm). With a pencil lightly draw a large heart shape in the center of the right side of one of the larger pieces of pink fabric. Paint the light pink paint directly onto a rubber stamp and print within the heart shape. Use all the rubber stamps to create a design inside the heart shape.

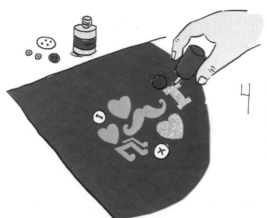

4 Paint over the stamped hearts with a layer of clear sparkly nail varnish. Sew on a selection of buttons and sequins in random places around the printed design.

5 Fold the top of each of the pink pieces of fabric over twice to the wrong side to create a hem and pin in place. Stitch along the top of the back piece with the sewing machine to hold the hem in place. On the front piece, pin the decorative trim across the top on the right side, securing the hem temporarily at the same time.

6 To make the handles, fold each of the fabric strips in half lengthwise with right sides together and machine stitch along the long edge. Turn the handles right way out and press.

7 Position the ends of one handle on the wrong side of the back of the bag at the top and about 2 in. (5 cm) in from each side. Pin in place. Machine a line of zigzag stitch across the top of the back piece, about ⅜ in. (1 cm) from the top edge to secure the handles. On the front piece position the handle in the same way, then zigzag stitch along the top and bottom of the trim to secure the trim, handles, and hem.

8 Place the front and back bag pieces right sides together and machine stitch along the two sides and the bottom edge. Turn the bag right side out and press. Sew the large fabric-covered button onto the front of the bag at the bottom of one handle end.

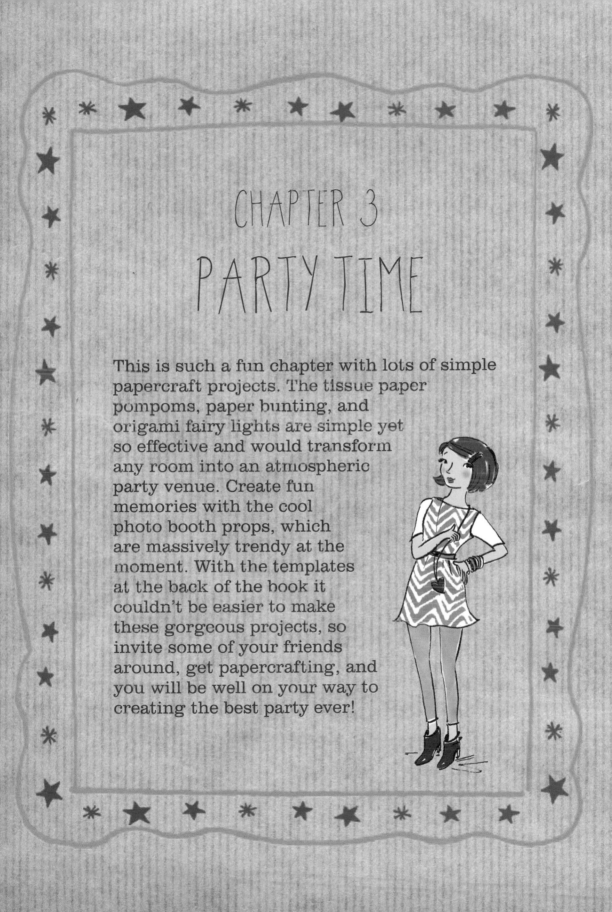

CHAPTER 3
PARTY TIME

This is such a fun chapter with lots of simple papercraft projects. The tissue paper pompoms, paper bunting, and origami fairy lights are simple yet so effective and would transform any room into an atmospheric party venue. Create fun memories with the cool photo booth props, which are massively trendy at the moment. With the templates at the back of the book it couldn't be easier to make these gorgeous projects, so invite some of your friends around, get papercrafting, and you will be well on your way to creating the best party ever!

PAPER BUNTING

Bunting is one of the easiest ways to instantly brighten up a room. Why not make this with your friends? If you all help out with cutting the triangles and sticking them together, the bunting will be finished in no time!

Skill Level ✂

YOU WILL NEED

Color photocopier and white paper

Scissors

60 in. (150 cm) ribbon

Two-hole punch

Glue or double-sided tape

1 Color photocopy and enlarge the patterned triangles from page 124. You will need 22 patterned triangles to create a bunting length of 11 triangles (60 in./150 cm long). Cut out each triangle shape.

2 Carefully, using the adhesive or double-sided tape, stick two triangles back to back with the printed side on the outside. Repeat for the rest of the triangles until you have 11 triangles that have a patterned front and back. Let dry.

3 Using the two-hole punch, make two holes at the top of each bunting triangle. Lay your patterned triangles out in the order in which you would like them to appear.

4 Tie a small knot at one end of the ribbon and then start to weave the other end in and out of the holes in the triangles until all triangles are on the ribbon. Tie a knot at the other end of ribbon to keep the triangles in place. Use sticky tack or invisible tape to hang the bunting on a wall or wherever you want to display it.

TIP

Patterned triangles are provided at the back of the book for you to photocopy and use, but if you see a design you like, on some giftwrap for example, why not use that instead? You can use one of our triangles as a template and stick the giftwrap onto thicker paper or cardstock to make it slightly sturdier.

BUTTON BADGES

Be a fashionista with these cute and quirky button badges! Choose from 12 badge designs at the back of the book. Wear the badges on your coat, school bag, scarf, or hat. The funky glasses or mad mustache badge will cheer up any dull outfit.

Skill Level ✂ ✂

YOU WILL NEED

Color photocopier
and white paper

Scissors

Badge maker containing
clear badge covers,
plastic badge inners,
plastic badge backs,
and plastic pin backs

1 Color photocopy the patterned circle badge templates on page 125. Cut around the outside of each patterned circle.

2 Place the circular clear badge cover in the bottom half of the badge maker. Add the patterned circle template on top, with the design side facing downward.

3 Add a badge inner inside the top section of the badge maker with the flat side facing downward. Close the badge maker and press down firmly.

TIP

The templates will create finished badges 1 in. (2.5 cm) in diameter—if your badge maker creates larger badges enlarge the templates on the photocopier to fit. The instructions on your badge maker may vary slightly from the ones given here—if so, follow the instructions that came with the badge maker.

4 Open the badge maker—the outer part of the clear badge cover and patterned circle template should have folded up all around the edge of the badge inner. If this has not completed successfully, use the tip of a finger to fold any excess paper in.

5 Place the badge back inside the top section of the badge maker. Close the badge maker and press down firmly until you hear the two parts of the badge click together. Alternatively you can just click the two sections together with your fingers.

6 Add the pin back on top of the badge back by pressing down hard and twisting it to the right to complete the badge. Repeat the steps to make more button badges.

FRIENDSHIP BRAIDS

Wow your friends with these contemporary and fresh twists on the friendship braid! Simple braiding techniques are combined with brass nuts, rivets, and gems to create fashionable accessories. If you make them with friends, you can help each other by holding the ends of the threads while the other braids.

Skill Level

Braided Brass Nut Bracelet
YOU WILL NEED

18 brass nuts (M4 or 4 mm size)

3 x 20-in. (50-cm) lengths beige stranded cotton

3 x 20-in. (50-cm) lengths bright pink stranded cotton

3 x 20-in. (50-cm) lengths lime green stranded cotton

BRAIDED BRASS NUT BRACELET

1. Tie all the lengths of cotton together in a knot at the top end. Using the safety pin, attach the knot to a cushion. Divide the threads into three bundles, making sure you have one thread of each color in each bundle. Number the thread bundles A, B, and C. Move bundle A into the center, over bundle B.

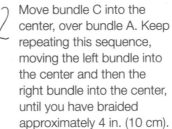

2. Move bundle C into the center, over bundle A. Keep repeating this sequence, moving the left bundle into the center and then the right bundle into the center, until you have braided approximately 4 in. (10 cm).

TIP
When braiding, you may find it easier to attach the safety pin to your pants leg.

3. Thread 6 nuts onto each bundle and carry on braiding as follows: each time you bring a bundle into the center, pull a nut up and secure into the braid. Repeat until all the nuts are in place, then continue to braid the remaining threads until the end. Tie a knot to secure.

RHINESTONE BRACELET

1 Fold all the threads in half and tie a knot
at the top. Using the safety pin, attach
the knot to a cushion. Arrange the
threads into two bundles so you have
three strands of each color in each
bundle. Begin the bracelet by criss-
crossing the first color (three strands)
over to the opposite side. Then cross
the same color from the other side.

2 Repeat with each color and a
chevron pattern will appear. Once
you have enough braid to wrap
around your wrist, tie a knot in the
end and trim the excess threads.

3 Lay the rhinestone chain
along the center of the braid
and stitch in place using
embroidery floss.

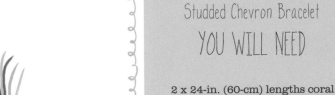

STUDDED CHEVRON BRACELET

1 Tie the ends of all the threads
together in a knot. Using the
safety pin, attach the knot to a
cushion. Arrange the threads so
the two coral strands are on the
outside, followed by one strand
of each color in the same order
from the outside to the center
on each side.

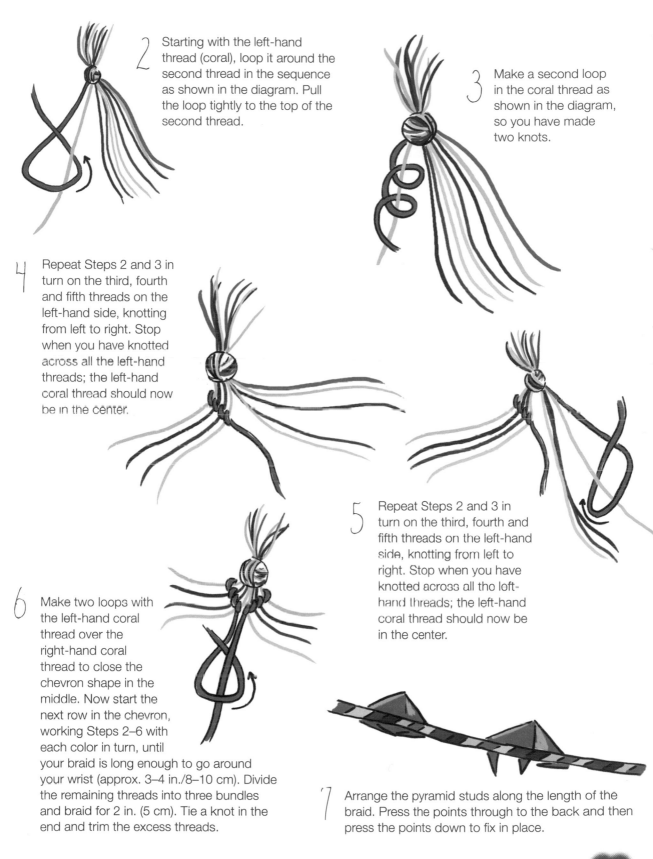

2 Starting with the left-hand thread (coral), loop it around the second thread in the sequence as shown in the diagram. Pull the loop tightly to the top of the second thread.

3 Make a second loop in the coral thread as shown in the diagram, so you have made two knots.

4 Repeat Steps 2 and 3 in turn on the third, fourth and fifth threads on the left-hand side, knotting from left to right. Stop when you have knotted across all the left-hand threads; the left-hand coral thread should now be in the center.

5 Repeat Steps 2 and 3 in turn on the third, fourth and fifth threads on the left-hand side, knotting from left to right. Stop when you have knotted across all the left-hand threads; the left-hand coral thread should now be in the center.

6 Make two loops with the left-hand coral thread over the right-hand coral thread to close the chevron shape in the middle. Now start the next row in the chevron, working Steps 2–6 with each color in turn, until your braid is long enough to go around your wrist (approx. 3–4 in./8–10 cm). Divide the remaining threads into three bundles and braid for 2 in. (5 cm). Tie a knot in the end and trim the excess threads.

7 Arrange the pyramid studs along the length of the braid. Press the points through to the back and then press the points down to fix in place.

INVITATIONS

Having a party? Why not make it more personal and create these simple invitations for all your friends and family? Everyone loves to receive a hand-crafted party invitation in the mail!

1 Color photocopy the invitation designs on pages 122–123. Repeat for the number of invitations you require. Cut out the front and back of each invitation.

2 Stick the front of the invitation to a piece of white cardstock with a thin layer of glue. Carefully cut out the front invitation close to the edge.

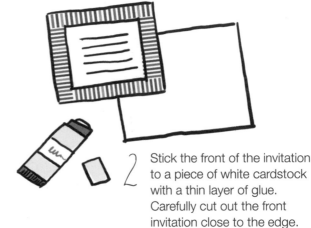

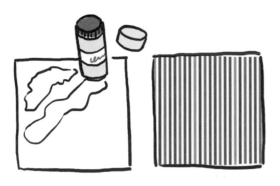

3 Turn the front of the invitation over and add a thin layer of glue to the back. Stick the back of the invitation onto the front.

4 Handwrite all your party information details in the area provided on the front side of the party invitation, using the marker pen. From top to bottom, the symbols stand for the date of the party, the time it starts, the address of the venue, your phone number, and your email address (so guests can reply to let you know if they're coming).

You may need some adult supervision for Step 5.

TIP
Why not decorate some plain envelopes to match the invitations?

5 Add a few gems to the outside edge of the invitation. If your gems are not self-adhesive, use a dab of glue from the hot glue gun. Once everything has dried, your invitations will be ready to send.

ORIGAMI FAIRY LIGHTS

Combine basic origami with fairy lights to create a magical glowing display that will look great at a party! Simply make origami balloons, then attach them to a string of lights.

1 With the colored side upward, fold the square in half vertically, open out and fold it horizontally, then open out again so you have two fold lines in the shape of a cross. Turn the sheet over and fold it in half diagonally both ways. Open the square out again.

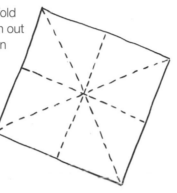

2 Turn the paper over and gently push the edges so the sheet folds along all the lines, with the diagonal folds coming up and the horizontal/vertical folds going down, to create a three-dimensional star shape.

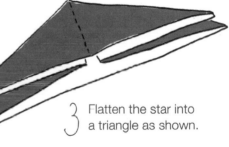

3 Flatten the star into a triangle as shown.

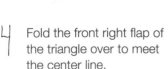

4 Fold the front right flap of the triangle over to meet the center line.

5 Repeat with the front left flap on the other side and then turn the triangle over and repeat for the right and left flaps on the other side to make a square sitting on one corner.

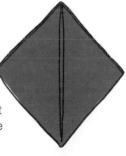

6 Fold the point of the right front flap over to the center line. Repeat with the left front flap. Turn the square over and repeat for the right and left flaps on the other side.

7 At the top of the shape you will still have four loose triangle flaps. Fold the top point of the left front flap down to make a smaller triangle.

8 Fold the whole triangle over again so it becomes a triangle flap on top of the left side triangle as made in Step 6.

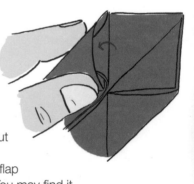

9 Unfold the last fold made. The side triangle underneath will have an opening along the top edge; open this out into a pocket and insert the triangle flap made in Step 8. You may find it easier to pop the pocket open with your thumb and forefinger before inserting the flap.

10 Repeat Steps 7–9 for the right front flap, then turn over and repeat for both sides on the back. Pull the four edges of the shape outward slightly.

11 At the base of the shape there will be a small hole. Gently blow into the hole and the shape will fill with air and puff out.

12 Make 19 more boxes in the same way. Insert an origami box over each light by pushing the light through the hole used to blow the box up.

CLAY GIFT TAGS

Air-dry or oven-bake clay is such an easy material to use. These gift tags are so pretty that they can make any gift look extra special with a handmade feel.

Cut a piece of brown cardboard 3¼ x 2⅜ in. (8 x 6 cm) and a piece of patterned paper 2¾ x 2 in. (7 x 5 cm) for each tag. Stick the patterned paper onto one side of the cardboard using the PVA glue. Cut two strips of graph paper each 2¾ x ⅜ in. (7 x 1 cm) and stick them onto the tag.

2 Punch a hole in the top of the tag with a hole punch. Fold the length of ribbon in half and feed the folded edge through the hole from back to front by about ¾ in. (2 cm). Put to one side until the clay decorations are ready.

3 Roll the clay out with the rolling pin so that it is approx. ¼ in. (0.5 cm) thick. Press stamps into the clay, leaving space around each design.

4 Use cookie cutters to cut out shapes around each stamped design. Use the tip of a pencil or a knitting needle to make a hole in the top of each clay decoration. Trim any excess clay with a knife to neaten the edges, and transfer the shapes to a clean baking sheet (tray).

5 Leave the clay shapes to air-dry or place them into the oven following the manufacturer's instructions, depending on the product you are using. When the clay shapes are hardened, paint in a selection of colors and allow to dry.

You may need some adult supervision for Step 5.

6 Thread the loop of ribbon on the cardboard tag through the hole in the clay decoration, and then thread the two loose ends of ribbon through the loop and pull tight. Handwrite your message onto the graph paper strips.

COLLAGE TREAT BAGS

These favor bags are a great way to give your guests a reminder of a fun party. Alternatively, they make great individual gift bags for presents—no two will be the same!

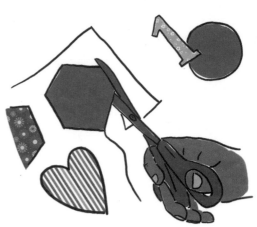

Skill Level

YOU WILL NEED

Color photocopier and white paper

Scissors

Ready-made brown paper sacks with handles

PVA glue or glue stick

Thin white cardstock

Scissors

Hole punch

Approx 6 in. (15 cm) of narrow ribbon for each sack

Stapler (optional)

Glitter, sequins, embroidery floss and needle (optional)

1 Color photocopy the treat bag images on pages 126–127. One copy will be enough for 2–3 paper sacks. Carefully cut out each shape.

2 Lay the cut out shapes onto the side of a brown paper sack. Move the shapes around until you are happy with how they look. Stick the shapes in place using PVA glue or a glue stick.

TIP
Use the badge-making instructions on page 96 to create decorations to pin to your bag for extra party style.

3 To create the hanging tag, stick one of the shapes to the white cardstock. Cut the shape out around the edge. Using a hole punch, punch a hole at the top center.

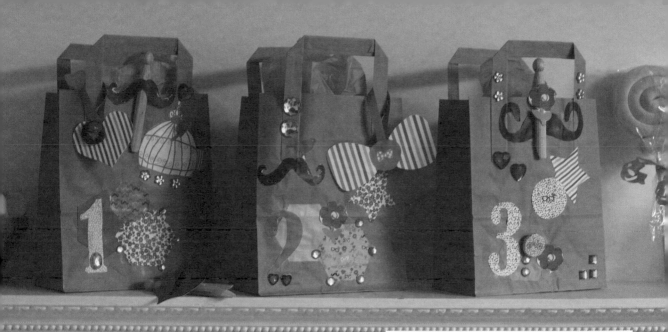

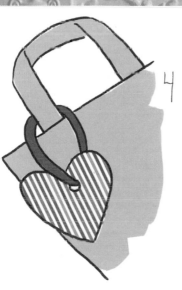

4 Thread a short length of ribbon through the punched hole, loop it around one handle of the sack and either tie into a bow or staple the ends to hold the tag in place.

5 Add glitter, sequins, or hand-stitched details to the treat bags as desired. Be creative and make up your own designs. Repeat for the other treat bags.

PHOTO BOOTH PROPS

No party is complete without photos, so let your guests get silly with these super photo booth props. You could personalize them by adding your favorite funny phrases on the speech bubble props.

Skill Level

YOU WILL NEED

Color photocopier and white paper

White cardstock

PVA glue

Scissors

Sequins in a variety of colors

Colored marker pen

Drinking straws

Adhesive tape

1 Color photocopy and enlarge the photo booth prop templates on page 120. Stick the copied sheet onto one side of the white cardstock using PVA glue.

2 Carefully cut around the outside edge of each of the shapes using sharp scissors.

3 Glue a few sequins around the outside edge of the speech bubbles, around the frame of the pink glasses, and on the center knot of the bow ties. Add wording of your choice to the speech bubbles using a colored marker pen.

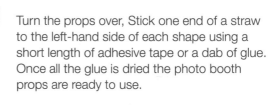

4 Turn the props over, Stick one end of a straw to the left-hand side of each shape using a short length of adhesive tape or a dab of glue. Once all the glue is dried the photo booth props are ready to use.

PAPER POMPOMS

These beautiful pompom decorations are perfect for a party, or why not simply hang them in your bedroom? They're really easy to make, so you could make one large pompom, or a set in different sizes, as seen here.

1 Take a set of 10 pieces of tissue paper and layer them on top of each other. Fold the layered tissue paper backward and forward into a concertina as if you were making a fan—for larger pompoms, each fold should be approx. 1½ in. (4 cm) wide, but this can be reduced for smaller pompoms. Crease each fold as you make it.

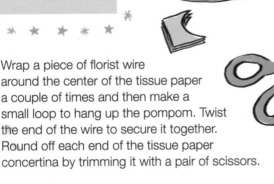

2 Wrap a piece of florist wire around the center of the tissue paper a couple of times and then make a small loop to hang up the pompom. Twist the end of the wire to secure it together. Round off each end of the tissue paper concertina by trimming it with a pair of scissors.

3 Open out each side of the tissue paper, then gently lift and separate all the layers to create a full pompom shape. Thread invisible thread through the wire loop and hang as desired. Repeat the steps to make each pompom.

TEMPLATES

This section contains all the templates you will need to make the projects in this book. Always read the labels carefully to check the size of the template you're using. Some of them are full-size templates and can be traced off the page; others are half-size templates, which means that you'll need to photocopy them at 200% to double the size of them. There is one template—the main bag piece for the Owl Fleece Tote—which is a quarter-size template and will need to be photocopied **twice** at 200% to make it the correct size.

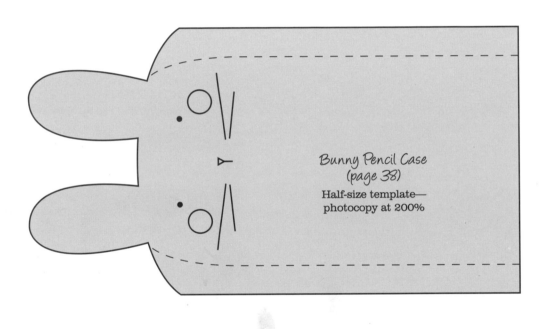

Bunny Pencil Case
(page 38)
Half-size template—
photocopy at 200%

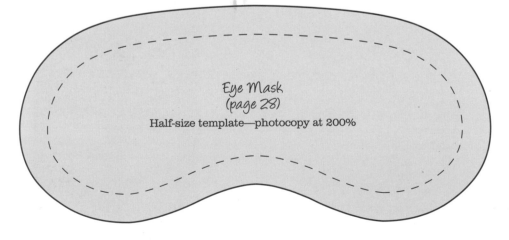

Eye Mask
(page 28)
Half-size template—photocopy at 200%

Felt Pencil Toppers
(page 47)
Full-size templates—trace and use at this size

Russian doll

Owl

Strawberry

Slipper Socks
(page 57)
Full-size templates—trace and use at this size

Inner eye

Outer eye

Nose

Stamps and Stamped Bag
(page 88)
Full-size templates—trace and use at this size
(For a heart-shaped stamp, use the panda nose from the Slipper Sock templates.)

I ♥ U

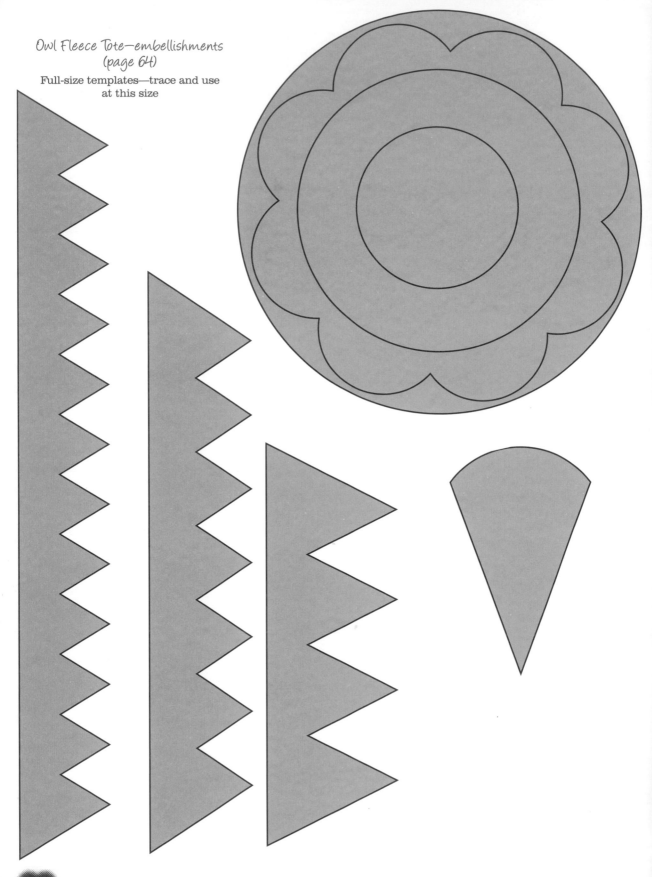

Owl Fleece Tote—embellishments
(page 64)

Full-size templates—trace and use
at this size

TEMPLATES

Owl Fleece Tote—main bag
(page 64)
Quarter-size template—photocopy at
200% to double the size, then photocopy
the enlarged copy at 200% again (if your
photocopier allows you to photocopy at
400%, you can do this instead and just
photocopy it once)

Pompom Flowers
(page 44)
Full-size template—
trace and use at this size

Felt iPod and Cellphone Cozy
(page 70)
Full-size templates—
trace and use at this size

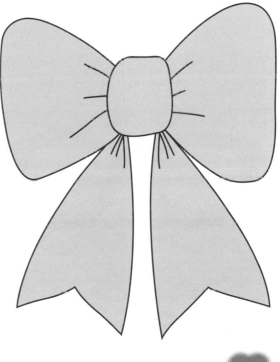

COLOR TEMPLATES

The following templates are patterned, so you will need to use a color photocopier to copy them. The button badges are full-size templates and can be photocopied at 100%; the others are half-size templates, which means that you'll need to photocopy them at 200% to double the size of them.

Photo Booth Props
(page 112)

Half-size templates—photocopy at 200%

Inside cover

Notebook
(page 74)
Half-size templates—photocopy at 200%

Outside cover

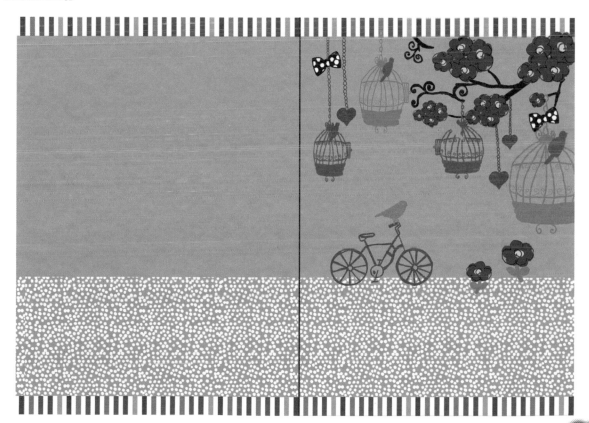

Invitations
(page 102)
Full-size templates

1	2	3
4	✗	6
7	8	9

Front

Back

Paper Bunting
(page 94)
Half-size templates—photocopy at 200%

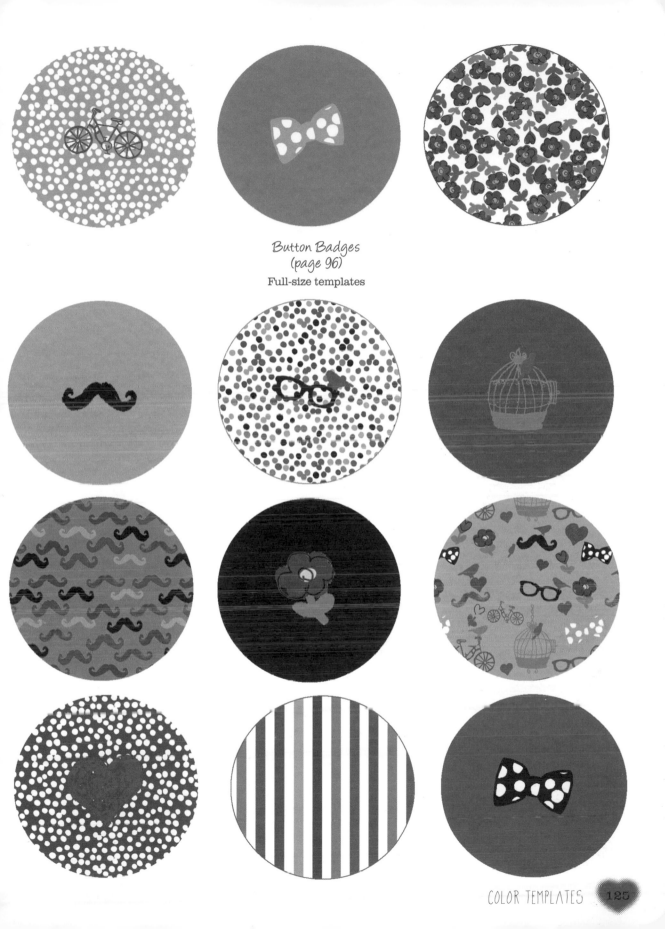

Button Badges
(page 96)
Full-size templates

Collage Treat Bags
(page 110)
Full-size templates